INDIA UNVEILED

Oh, East is East, and West is West, and never the twain shall meet,
Till Earth and Sky stand presently at God's great Judgment Seat;
But there is neither East nor West, border, nor breed, nor birth,
When two strong men stand face to face, though they come from the ends of the earth!

Rudyard Kipling
The Ballad of East and West, 1889

INDIA UNVEILED

Text and Photographs
by
Robert Arnett

All photographs by Robert Arnett unless otherwise indicated.

Atman Press 1996

Published by Atman Press, 2525 Auburn Avenue, Box 345,
Columbus, Georgia 31906.

Book manufacturer: Sung In Printing America, 465 Forbes Boulevard,
South San Francisco, California 94080.

Printed and bound in Korea.

FIRST EDITION
Publisher's Cataloging-in-Publication Data
Arnett, Robert, 1942 -
INDIA UNVEILED/Text and Photographs by Robert Arnett
215 p. 31 cm.
Includes glossary and index
ISBN: 0-9652900-7-7

1. India—Description and travel. 2. India—Social life and customs.
3. Art—India. 4. Architecture—India. 5. Photography— India. 6. Religion and Culture—India.

DS421.A76 1996
915.4-dc20   Library of Congress Catalog Card Number: 96-85065

ACKNOWLEDGEMENTS FOR ILLUSTRATIONS

All photographs are by Robert Arnett except those appearing on the following pages:

Mr. Ashok Dilwali, Kinsey Brothers, A-2 Connaught Place, New Delhi, India 110001. Pages 80, 104, 106-107. (General Photographs of India)

Mr. Debasish Mukherjee, 91/U Joykissen Street, P.O. Uttarpara, Hooghly, West Bengal, India 712258. Page 105. (Nature photographs and commissions)

Mr. Syed Ali Shah, Post Office Ley, Ladakh, India 194101. Page 121. (Photographs of Ladakh)

Mr. Jay Waronker, Atlanta, Georgia. Top photograph on page 191. (Synagogues of India)

Mr. Scott McIntyre, c/o Atman Press, 2525 Auburn Avenue, Box 345, Columbus, Georgia 31906. (Maps)

7 8 9 0 1 2 3 4 5 6   12 11 10 9 8 7 6 5 4 3 2

Dedication

This book is dedicated to the memory of Paramahansa Yogananda, author of Autobiography of a Yogi, *and the other great masters of India. Through the ages they have renounced all worldly possessions and dedicated their lives to bring to the followers of all faiths the sacred liberating science of yoga, by which the soul may be merged back into the One.*

Author's Notes and Acknowledgements

On a business trip to Detroit, Michigan in 1969, I met a young man at an ex ibition of Far Eastern Art. Our conversation turned to a discussion of Indian philosophy, about which I had very little knowledge. The exchange intrigued me, and as I would realize later, I was at a crossroads on my life's journey. My new acquaintance suggested that I read <u>Autobiography of a Yogi</u>. He then invited me to accompany him to a yoga service the following Sunday. My first meditation experience brought me to a level of consciousness which I had never known. It was the impetus which led to my in-depth study of Indian philosophy and the sacred science of Kriya Yoga, an ancient meditation technique whose devoted practice leads to direct, personal experience of God. The more I learned the more I sought to know. I felt very strongly that I needed to return to a place I had never been; and in December of 1988, destiny set my path toward India. Without itinerary or expectations, I began the first of three solitary journeys, each of which would last for six months. It was during that short span of time on my second trip that my life was transformed. Not only was the Indian subcontinent unveiled to me, but in the process, I discovered the true essence of my being.

This book is a tribute to the traditional values of India. For thousands of years, the basic cornerstones of Indian culture had changed very little, and probably account for why some historians believe India to be the oldest continuously surviving civilization on earth.

Modern India, like the rest of the world, is in a state of major transition as her people grapple with the enormous task required to balance science and modern technology with the inner peace of the soul. Although Indian culture has had the resiliency to withstand over 300 years of Mughal conquest, I wondered if it could survive the effects of Western materialism on its growing middle class. I now know that my concerns were unfounded. My travels throughout India revealed that Hindu values are deeply ingrained in its society. Not only will India be able to assimilate Western technology into its own culture, but will be stronger for it. Long after the modern buildings in cosmopolitan Bombay have been reduced to rubble by time and the elements, the eternal verities of village India will be as vibrant as ever.

I am deeply indebted to Gail B. Greenblatt for the numerous editing hours spent with me. Her contribution was truly a labor of love. Her feel for the language and syntactical skill made a rambling manuscript readable.

To Professor Roy C. Craven Jr., I am grateful not only for his writing the Preface, but also for kindling my initial desire to go to India.

To Dr. C. Selvaraj, Madras Christian College, Madras, India for reading the manuscript and making invaluable suggestions and corrections.

To Dr. S. Mitra of Emory University, Atlanta, Georgia for his encouragement and support.

To Thom Hendrick of Xpress Printing, Columbus, Georgia for digital design and helping lay out the book.

To Wayne Turner, Managing Director, Sung In Printing America, New York for supervising the printing of the book.

To my mother for her helpful suggestions and faith. Every son should have the joy of sharing something so dear to his heart with his mother.

Robert A. Arnell

July 25, 1996

Preface

By Roy C. Craven Jr.*
Professor of Indian Art History, Emeritus
University of Florida, Gainesville
Author of <u>A Concise History of Indian Art</u>, Thames and Hudson · London

Ever since Alexander the Great came out of the mountain passes of Afghanistan onto the plains of North India in 326 B.C., Westerners have been reacting and recording their impressions of the rich, multi-hued culture of India.

The narrative which follows is a remarkable accounting of one American's rigorous pilgrimage across India to confirm his spirituality and to search out India's reality. This intense journey takes Robert Arnett from Gujarat and the sands of the Thar desert in the west — to Calcutta and Bhubaneswar in the east — to the extreme southern tip of the subcontinent at Rameswaram and Kanyakumari — to the icy visions of the high Himalayas seen from Darjeeling and Kashmir — and, along the way, to the numerous, ancient and remarkable sacred sites, of the genre only to be found in India.

Robert Arnett's journey is defined by his explorations for the sacred in great modern cities and in small villages as well as in the remote shrines and ashrams of gurus and swamis. This is achieved by traveling nights and days on trains and crowded country buses.

Through it all the traveler has preserved for the reader a complex collage of scenes, sounds and personalities which coalesce into a mosaic of Indian land and personalities — and along the way the pilgrim and his quest are revealed as well.

This is a narrative of feeling and devotion which will move the reader by its rich scope and emotion.

It is with deep regret that we note that Professor Craven died in June, 1996.

Contents

An Homage to India

Bob Arnett's love affair with India began 25 years ago. The images portrayed on the following pages are exotic and touchingly human. Arnett's narrative creates for the reader the same intensity and adventure with which he himself has pursued India. The photographs exude his fascination of both ancient and contemporary India and its intriguing places he traversed with a singular devotion of a pilgrim in search of some kind of salvation. With his panoramic lens, he captures the very soul of India, revealing the splendor and antiquity of India's heritage, thus trapping India's scintillating beauty and spiritual depths for all to see.

India has always been a photographer's paradise, and Arnett's work has provided an opportunity for the world to rediscover India — offering an epic glimpse into the ethos of one of the world's most vibrant and culturally rich civilizations — earlier and preeminent to Greek and Roman civilizations. The places of worship and the artistic treasures created by artisans and craftsmen of different cultural persuasions have been portrayed with deep sensitivity. This meticulous compilation is bound to awaken a sense of pride for people of Indian origin and also encourage them to learn more about their roots. For others, India Unveiled is an invitation to share an Indian experience through the eyes of a Westerner, who has created an ambiance replete with India's heritage, history, folklore and culture.

As we commemorate India's 50th anniversary of Independence, India Unveiled is a befitting tribute to a country that has been a beacon for spirituality. It is indeed an honor for me to be part of an homage to the people of India, and I congratulate Mr. Robert Arnett for having presented India in a most colorful, beautiful and spiritual way to the world. India Unveiled is simply divine!

Subash Razdan
President
National Federation of Indian American Associations, NFIA
Atlanta, Georgia, USA
October 25, 1996

A Culture of Sharing

India's has always been a culture of sharing. This is why it has continued to grow from the earliest times, changing but never broken. Although we may not be the world's oldest civilization, therefore, we are indeed the oldest living civilization. As Stuart Cary Welch of the Metropolitan Museum, New York, says in his <u>India: 1300 - 1900</u>:

> Ancient India is with us still, direct and palpable, as is no other early civilization.

This is typified by the worship of the Lord Shiva, premier deity of the Hindu pantheon, whose origin lies in the Indus Valley civilization, predating even the advent of the Aryans, dating to about 5,000 B.C. But the foundation of the Indian cultural heritage can be traced to the days of the Rig Veda, the holy book developed by the earliest Aryans in about 2,000 to 1,500 B.C., who are also the earliest recorded immigrants. This work continues to be among the holiest of Hindu scriptures, but even if not recognized by other faiths as scripture, lays down certain principles which continue to govern Indian thought and action. I mention but two: One is the concept of *Vasudhaiva Kutumbakam*, humankind as one family. The world for us is therefore one and we can relate with any people anywhere in the world; they are not alien to us nor we to them. The second concept is that God is one, even though the paths to Him might be many. This is the foundation of our secular ideals and also the reason why people who are not Hindu by faith can be equal adherents of these lessons.

After the Aryans, India saw a number of immigrations: "Wave upon wave of ethnically and linguistically varied people eventually laid down their arms, settled and were assimilated." We had the Greeks, known to us as the Yavanas, the Yueh Chi, known as the Kushanas, the Scythians or Sakas, the Huns, whom we called the Hunas, the Gujjars, Arabs, Turks, Jats and Mongols. All of them brought something into our country which merged with the rest, and they in turn absorbed the Indian heritage. To take but illustrative examples, the Greek contribution is easily traceable in traditional sculpture, specifically what we call the Gandhara School. Chinese and Persian styles of painting were brought in by the Moghuls and became a distinctive part of the Moghul, Rajput and Kangra styles. <u>India Unveiled</u> places before the reader much that will inform and fascinate.

Robert Arnett has rendered a signal service in presenting India in all her richness and diversity to the American public to relish and to savour. Naturally, in a work of this kind there will be many views and opinions on how this diversity may be perceived. Robert Arnett has seen these through the eyes of a friendly beholder.

Naresh Chandra
Ambassador of India
Washington, D.C.
October 25, 1996

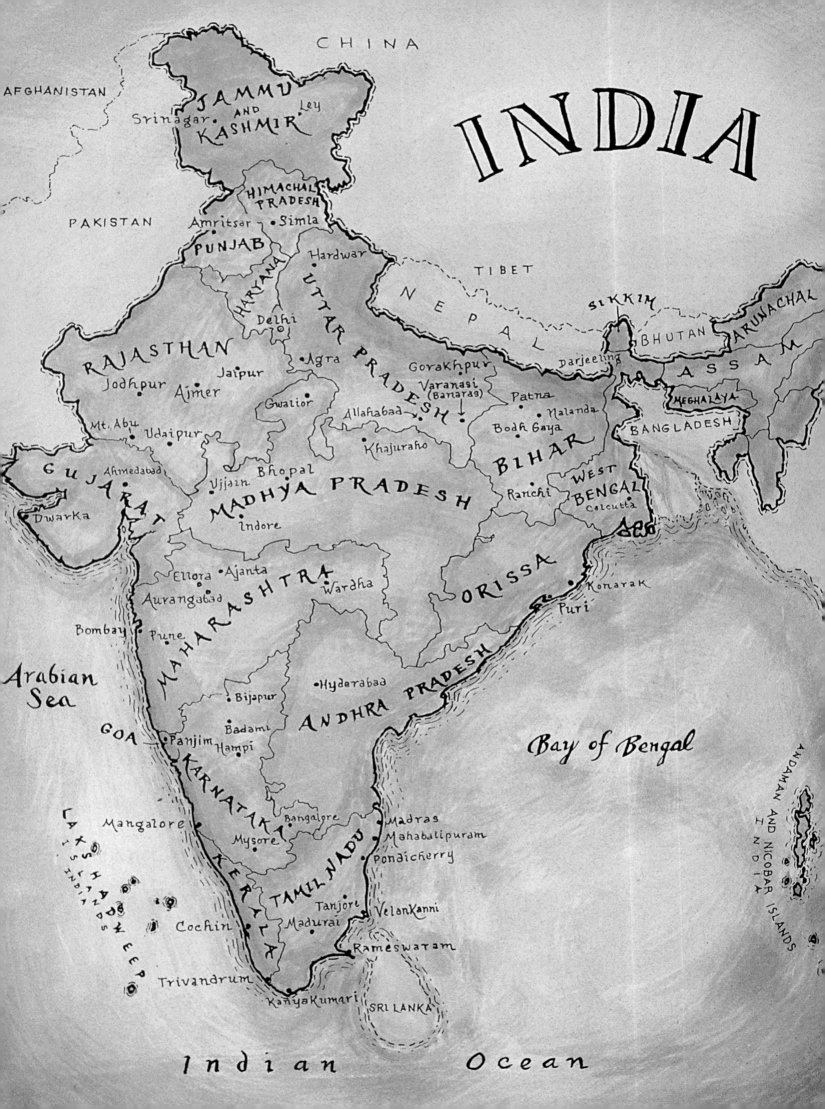

Introduction

For those unfamiliar with India and her customs, I would like to share some background. The term Indians applies equally to Hindus, Muslims, Christians, Sikhs, Jains, Buddhists, Parsis, Jews or anyone who is a citizen of India (and through the geographical error of Christopher Columbus, to the aboriginals of the Americas). The name Hindu came from the Greeks who invaded northwestern India under Alexander the Great. They designated the inhabitants of the banks of the Indus River as Indoos, or Hindus. The word Hindus refers only to the followers of Hinduism, the name given to the collection of the ancient scriptures of India, the Vedic teachings, whose four books are known as India's *Sanatana Dharma*, Eternal Religion. Unless a minority religion is mentioned by name, the reader may assume that the text refers to the Hindu people or their culture.

With almost one billion inhabitants who live in a space about one-third the size of the United States, India is the world's largest democracy. It has the second largest population in the world, ranking behind China. India is still overwhelmingly rural and its economy is predominantly agricultural. Even with its immense population, India is able to feed its people without having to import food. Although it has over 20 cities with a population of more than a million and is one of the world's major industrial powers, about 70 percent of the population still lives in rural areas. In the villages, life is unhurried and only changing seasons mark the passing of time. There is still widespread poverty, but with an affluent middle class of over 200 million people, India is fast becoming one of the largest markets for consumer goods in the world, hardly an image to fit most Western stereotypes of the subcontinent.

Cultural Diversity

The diversity of Indian religions accounts for much of its cultural richness. Its ancient Hindu legacy intertwines with monuments from Jain, Buddhist, Mughal, Sikh, Christian and the British Raj period. There was even a Jewish presence in Cochin in South India which probably dated back to the time of King Solomon's merchant fleets. Their descendants have intermarried with the Hindu population. Although there is only a handful of Jews remaining in Cochin today, a 16th century synagogue, said to be the oldest in the British Commonwealth, still exists. Built by European Jews, many of whom came from Spain after the Inquisition, its congregation once numbered about 4,000.

The reader should note that even within India's state boundaries, there are a myriad of ethnological differences which include languages, customs and foods. Because of such a diverse population, India has been referred to as a "continent within a country."

Despite these distinctions, the Indian government has managed to foster a national consciousness. This probably would not have been possible without the resiliency of the social and religious institutions of Hinduism which are still intact after thousands of years. One of the great challenges to the Indian government at the national, state and local levels is to solve the increasingly transnational public issues of their diverse, multicultural population. That India has faced, endured and absorbed far greater confrontations in the past offers hope for a harmonious and prosperous future.

Languages

National homogeneity is virtually unknown, which is not surprising in a country with no "Indian" language. Fifteen languages are recognized by the Constitution, and over 700 minor dialects are spoken. On most Indian currency, thirteen languages are printed! Most of the major languages have their own alphabet. Amongst the Indian population, this diversity can be confusing. To a Westerner, like myself, it sometimes can become downright embarrassing. By far, my greatest misreading of a posted sign was in the Himalayan Mountain region known as "The Valley of the Gods." While seeking a place to put on my bathing suit at a hot springs in Manali, I mistakenly entered the women's changing room. It made me realize how careful I needed to be with so many languages and dialects bombarding me each day. Even trying to decipher Indian body language could be perplexing. In parts of India, if someone shook his head horizontally from side to side, this mannerism meant "yes."

Absence of a national language partially accounts for the fact that English is still widely used almost 50 years after India received its independence from the British. Tour guides often routinely spoke English in addressing Indians from other regions. In Parliament, where many top officials still address their colleagues in English, major efforts have been made to promote Hindi as the national language, though it is only spoken as the Mother tongue by about 20 percent of the population. Although the Indo-Aryan language of Hindi is spoken predominantly in the north, it has little similarity to the Dravidian languages of the south, that were introduced into that region thousands of years ago. Considering the distinct and proud cultural legacy of the south, which was never conquered by Mughal invaders, opposition to Hindi is not unexpected and naturally conflicts arise.

The school systems in most states in India teach three languages: English, Hindi and the vernacular of that particular state or region. In addition, some students learn the ancient Sanskrit, the classical literary language of the Indian scriptures which is the world's oldest surviving language. Even Western linguists agree that Sanskrit (which consists of fifty letters, each one having a fixed, invariable pronunciation that prevents mispronunciations) is the most perfect phonetic language in the world. George Bernard Shaw agreed. He wrote a wise and witty essay urging the adoption of a new English alphabet with an additional sixteen characters, which would approximate the phonetic perfection of Sanskrit, even if "it cost a civil war!" Because of Sanskrit's pleasing sound and meter, I usually could distinguish it from the local dialects or from Hindi. Often, when hearing Sanskrit prayers, it would evoke a tingling sensation within me, as if it was resonating in my inner core. My finding someone who spoke English was seldom a problem, although there were times on local country buses when no one knew English and I had to fend for myself. Even when sign language failed, I never got off at the wrong destination.

Religion

India has possibly a greater diversity of religions and sects than anywhere else in the world. It is the birthplace of Hinduism, Buddhism, Jainism and Sikhism, and is an important home to Zoroastrianism, one of the world's oldest surviving religions.

Hinduism, India's majority religion, is practiced by about 80 percent of the population. It is difficult to define the religion. It has been said that every metaphysical thought that ever was, is or ever will be — has already been expressed in India. Hinduism contains various approaches to achieve its ultimate goal, oneness with God, and it could take a lifetime of study just to master even one of its many aspects. Hinduism's earliest scriptures are the Vedas. These texts were passed down orally, and were only transcribed during the last millennium. The corpus of the religion's sacred writings also include the ancient allegories, the Mahabharata and Ramayana, the world's longest epic poems. Their complex symbolism represents the physical, mental and spiritual battles that each of us must fight and win in our daily lives. Contained within the Mahabharata is the Bhagavad Gita, "Song of the Spirit," the Hindu Bible which is the most beloved and sacred scripture of India. Its verses recount the sublime wisdom given by Lord Krishna to his disciple, Prince Arjuna. Hinduism embraces the doctrine of reincarnation, which declares that our unfulfilled material desires force us to return again and again to earth until we consciously attain oneness with God. Even the early Christian Church accepted the principle of reincarnation, although this doctrine was declared a heresy in 553 A.D. by the Second Council of Constantinople.

Hinduism is greatly misunderstood in the West. Most occidentals do not realize that Hinduism is a monotheistic belief in only one God, who as Creator is beyond time, space and physical form. The entire pantheon of Hindu gods and goddesses are merely symbolic representations of different attributes of the One, Unmanifested Spirit.

Hinduism created a different deity for each of God's numerous qualities to make God seem more real and approachable. I noticed that in the villages, many female followers of Lord Krishna preferred to worship him in the form of a baby rather than as a man, no doubt because it made it easier for them to share their maternal feelings for the Lord.

Hinduism is a very tolerant religion. It does not claim exclusivity of the true God only for itself. One of the Hindu scriptures, the Rig Veda, clearly states: "Though men call it by many names, it is really One." Hinduism also acknowledges that God took many human embodiments on earth, to include the saviors of other religions. A Divine incarnation is called an *avatar*, one who has attained union with Spirit and then returns to earth to help humankind. He is Divinity who has descended into flesh. Hindus consider Christ to be an *avatar*, but believe God also took form in other saviors such as Krishna and Buddha. A Hindu sage and poet wrote, "...I know Thou hast delighted, and wilt ever delight, in revealing Thyself in different forms....but Thou hast only one Nature: Perennial Joy."[1] Hindus also recognize the Divine inspiration of prophets such as Moses and Mohammed.

Muslims are India's largest minority. Though they comprise only about 12 percent of the population, they account for the largest Muslim population anywhere in the world outside of Indonesia. They believe that the Koran, the sacred scripture of Islam, contains revelations that were given directly to Mohammed by Allah (God). Islam shares common origins with Judaism, including the belief that creation began with Adam and that Ibrahim (Abraham) is an important prophet. The religion also recognizes as prophets Nuh (Noah), Musa (Moses) and Isa (Jesus).

Sikhs number a little over one percent of India's population. Traditionally, they do not cut their hair, smoke tobacco or drink alcohol, and the men are easily recognizable by the distinctive style of their turbans and thick, full beards. The holy city of Amritar, the Sikhs' Mecca, is located in the northwestern Indian state of the Punjab, close to the border of Pakistan. The Golden Temple, the Sikhs' holiest shrine, is located there. The religion was founded in 1469 by Guru Nanak, who was revered by both Hindus and Muslims. He espoused the best of both religions and made a conscious attempt to harmonize these two most powerful rival religions of India.

Descriptions of Buddhism, Jainism and Zoroastrianism will be discussed in their respective chapters.

Devotion

When I am asked what impressed me most about India, my reply is the peaceful demeanor of her people and their openly expressed devotion. The following story will illustrate both characteristics. After a four hour bus journey from Madras to the South Indian town of Tirupathi, our guide informed us that we would not be able to continue our trip to the nearby holy mountain of Tirumala. A local labor strike prevented our going further. Because Tirumala is one of the more important pilgrimage centers in all of India, the passengers were very disappointed, yet none complained. Most were tranquil as we sat together in a group waiting to see what would transpire. We realized that missing our visit to the magnificent statue of Sri Balaji, the deity to whom the temple was dedicated, would be a great loss to us all. Hindus believe that prayer requests made standing before this statue will be granted, which explains why an average of 30,000 pilgrims visit there on any given day. I struck up a conversation with one of the passengers who saw the labor strike as a man-made adversity that could serve as a spiritual challenge for all of us. His insight inspired me and I joined the others in praying silently that our pilgrimage to Tirumala would somehow be completed. At that moment such peace came over me that I had no doubt that God would grant our request. Shortly after lunch, we were told that the strike had been canceled and the buses would transport us to the mountaintop. Through God's grace, I had been able to tap into the collective devotion of the pilgrims and to feel their all-pervasive love, which I believe changed the course of events. I learned a great lesson that day: Prayer is more powerful than protest!

In a similar situation in other countries, most people would have complained vehemently. But not these pilgrims. Because of the value and historical proof in Indian life that prayer has worked for millenniums, there was no discussion and it was a given that prayer was the natural and proper course of action. More than in any other culture I know, Hindus have connected God with their daily life.

Hindus' deep devotion to God, especially amongst women, seemed to me to be inborn. At most temples, when the services were over, a priest carried a flaming oil lamp among the worshipers. The flame symbolized that God is Light, and most persons present would pass their hands above the sacred lamp and touch their forehead in reverence for God's presence. The women in the temple usually rushed forward to receive the sacrament with such childlike enthusiasm that it was as if God were actually there.

Another revealing incident took place while I was traveling in the modern city of Bangalore. I visited one of its oldest temples, known as the "Bull Temple," which is named after a huge monolithic sculpture of Shiva's Bull, Nandi. A little boy standing in front of the altar was too short to see the image of the deity. He kept tugging on his mother's sari until she could ignore him no longer. When she lifted him up for a peek, he leaned over and lovingly kissed the statue. The child's adoration was not unique, and I witnessed similar occurrences at several other shrines.

I remembered the comments of a Hindu doctor whom I had visited in Western India. He told me that "Because of the devotional nature of the Hindu people, the foremost thoughts of the mother and the father are of God. This devotion manifests itself within the mother's womb during pregnancy through the influences of the parents' conscious and subconscious thoughts, and when the child is born, devotion is part of its nature."

Devotion expressed itself outwardly in various ways, including the strong sense of responsibility that individuals exhibited for their parents and members of their extended family. A man I sat next to while traveling told me a poignant story. His mother had been in a coma in a Bombay hospital. Against all hospital regulations, the man's wife insisted on staying in the same room and even slept on the floor to be close to her mother-in-law, ensuring that she was timely bathed and kept in clean clothing. Doctors and even her husband's relatives told his wife that his mother would not survive. But against all odds, she did! His mother had a total recovery and now lives happily again with her son and daughter-in-law. He commented: "Loving feelings can save a life."

The deep loyalty that exists between husbands and wives and other family members serves as a living example from one generation to another. An Indian doctor whom I had met told me that his father, a man of modest means, had paid his college expenses. The doctor, who had a large practice said, "I am a doctor and a man today because of what my father sacrificed for me. If my father ever needed me, I would close my practice, withdraw my children from school, even if it meant their missing important exams, and take my family the several hundred miles to my father's home to care for him. I would not allow a servant to touch my father in my presence." To bathe and otherwise assist his father was the doctor's pleasure and duty. His children would see him serve his father, and in turn they would serve their father, and their children would serve them. The elderly die peacefully in India, surrounded by their devoted families, and in the familiar setting of their own homes. They have a "soft" death and pass on fulfilled. To me, this is the quiet beauty of India.

After visiting with many Indian families over a period of years, I am impressed by the sincerity with which each family member accepts his or her familial responsibilities. Duties were not discharged from a sense of obligation as if they were burdensome. An Indian I met on a bus explained that "Duty is performed from love and affection, like a mother taking care of her child." He said his mother and wife still serve in that spirit. Though there was some inconvenience caused from three generations living together in his home, he stated that his wife did not feel burdened by a house full of people and seemed to thrive on her selfless duties. He was emphatic that "Action must be supported by feeling. Once it becomes a duty performed mechanically without feeling, the tradition ends!"

I do not suggest that Indians or any peoples of third world countries should deny themselves the material benefits of Western civilization, yet, it seems to me that many young Indians (as well as the youth in much of the rest of the world) are forgetting the true values of the family structure. The attributes of duty, loyalty and service are often forsaken in favor of selfish considerations and monetary gain. Many are moving away from their ancestral homes, opting to live even in the slums of cities or moving to other countries, in search of treasures without value.

As the twentieth century draws to a close and a new millennium is about to begin, it is my hope and prayer that all of us will do our part to strengthen our individual families, and by extension, the family of man.

Righteous Action (*Dharma*)

It is impossible to understand India unless one understands the concept of *dharma*. *Dharma* has many meanings to the Hindu. No single English word can summarize all of its connotations. Within an individual's own life, it refers to one's inherent duty to live in harmony with the eternal principles of righteousness that uphold all creation. Thus, the social and moral implications of the Indian philosophy of *dharma* are reflected in the highest virtues expected from each member of the community. It is seen most clearly in village India. I recall once in a small town in Rajasthan, a young boy saw me drop my wallet which contained a huge sum of money by his standard. When he came up to me to return it, I tried to offer him a few rupees, but he would accept nothing. I asked someone nearby to explain to the boy why I wanted to give him something for his act of honesty. After talking to him, the man explained to me that the concept of accepting a gift for doing a good deed made no sense to the child. *Dharma* is a noble act and needed no outside reward.

The Guest Is God

Though I come from an area of the United States where people pride themselves on their "Southern hospitality," it could not compare to the gracious treatment I received in India. There is a beautiful Hindu story about the archangel, Narada, whom God sent to earth incognito to see who was worthy of a visit from The Most High, Himself. I was treated so thoughtfully in all of the homes I visited, whether rich or poor, that it was as if people considered me to be Narada. I learned quickly to limit my compliments for any objects I might see in an Indian home, as my hosts were quick to offer me almost anything I admired. The Indians' willingness to give away their prized belongings prompted me to examine the value system of my own country, where the need to acquire more and more "stuff" is a major goal of life. In the Bhagavad Gita, Lord Krishna emphasizes the importance of non-attachment to things of the physical world. If one does not carefully distinguish between the soul and the ego, then one's physical and spiritual focus is directed outward toward the object of temporary values. In the end, all worldly things return to dust, but the soul can return to God.

India's Gift to the World

India's spiritual heritage is legendary. Throughout the millenniums, India has been blessed with more masters — persons who during their lives on earth have merged their souls with God — than any other country in the world. There are many well-documented stories of their miracles. The famous master Trailanga Swami, who lived in Banaras during the late 19th century, displayed miraculous powers that cannot be dismissed as myth. Until recently, there were living witnesses to his amazing feats. Many persons witnessed him drink the most deadly poisons with no ill effect. Thousands of people saw him levitating in a sitting position on the surface of the Ganges for days at a time. He would even disappear under the waves for long periods, finally to reappear unharmed. Though Trailanga seldom ate, he weighed over 300 pounds. The yogi never wore any clothing and was arrested by the police for his nudity on several occasions, and locked in a cell. Each time, even with posted guards, he unexplainably escaped and could be seen walking on the prison roof, his cell still locked. The police had no clue as to how he did it.

For over 2,300 years, travelers from the most powerful countries on earth have come to India in search of her priceless spiritual wisdom. When Alexander the Great returned to Persia after his unsuccessful invasion of India, the most valued treasure that he brought back with him was not gold, jewels, silks or spices — but his guru (spiritual teacher), the yogi Kalyana, called "Kalanos" by the Greeks.

On a designated day in Susa, Persia, the sage Kalanos gave up his aged body by entering a funeral pyre in view of the entire Macedonian army. The soldiers were amazed that the yogi had no fear of pain or death and never once moved from his position as he was being consumed by flames. Kalanos embraced many of his close companions before leaving for his cremation but refrained from bidding farewell to Alexander, to whom he simply remarked: "I shall see you later in Babylon." Alexander died a year later in Babylon. The Indian guru's prophecy was his way of saying that he would be with Alexander both in life and death.

When the Chinese traveler Hieuen Tsiang attended a huge religious gathering, the *Kumbha Mela*, in Allahabad in 544 A.D., he recounts that Harsha, king of Northern India, gave away the entire wealth of his royal treasury to monks and pilgrims attending the event. When Hieuen Tsiang prepared to return to China, he declined Harsha's offerings of jewels and gold. Understanding that his spiritual development was more valuable than worldly wealth, he accepted, instead, 657 religious manuscripts. Likewise, through the science of yoga, India has given the West a far more valuable gift than all the material wealth or technology the West could give in return. Even today, India offers great inspiration to those persons who are seeking a oneness with God, and through yoga anyone can find the direction he or she needs to succeed. That is India's gift to the world.

Early morning haze over Hindu temples and the ruins of a 17th century palace. Orchha, Madhya Pradesh.

Chapter One

Central India

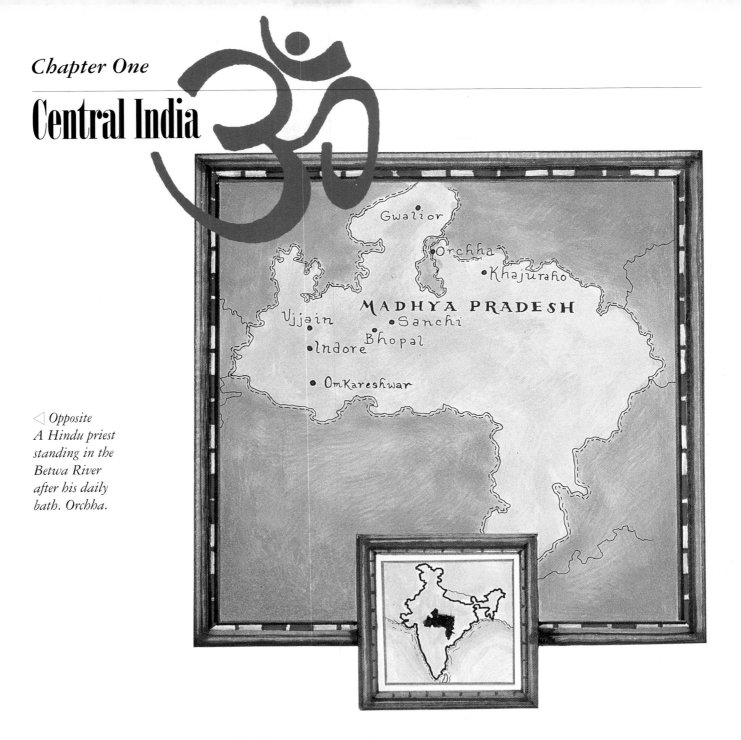

◁ *Opposite*
A Hindu priest
standing in the
Betwa River
after his daily
bath. Orchha.

State of Madhya Pradesh

India is comprised of 25 separate states and seven territories. Madhya Pradesh is the largest state and the geographical heartland of the country. Much of this state is located on a high plateau and like most of India, it can be uncomfortably hot and dry in summer. Most Western travelers only visit this part of India to see its famous temples at Khajuraho, known for their erotic carvings. But the state does have several other towns that are among my favorites in all of India. The great Buddhist masterpiece at Sanchi with its rich iconography of elephants, solar discs and scenes from the Buddha's life should not be missed. Omkareshwar, the pure and unspoiled sacred Hindu island replete with humble village pilgrims and boats with upturned bows, also is well worth a visit. Both of these magnificent sites are remote and can only be reached by local buses.

Sunrise silhouettes 17th century palaces built during Orchha's golden age.

Orchha

One of the least visited, but most picturesque places in all of India is Orchha. Today it is just a quiet village, but in the 17th century it was the capital of a powerful Rajput kingdom whose golden age included a palace especially built for the Mughal emperor Jehangir. Many of the town's splendid palaces have survived the centuries in excellent condition, and because so few tourists visit the isolated area, it was as if I had somehow stepped back into that colorful era myself. Being able to stay in one of the few rooms at the Hotel Sheesh Mahal, located in a wing of the Jehangir palace, was an additional delight. It surely must be the most romantic place to stay in Madhya Pradesh. I will always remember the view from my room after waking up early one morning and going to the window to open the shutters. This mist rising from the meandering river cast a haze over the rural countryside. Spired Hindu temples surrounded by patches of verdant grasses, and ruins of a small palace looked more like a scene from the chateau country of France than Central India. For the briefest moment I thought that I must be dreaming. I grabbed my camera and rushed to the roof-top to capture this ethereal scene. Considering the well-preserved palaces, the regal simplicity of my hotel and savory Indian cuisine, I could not have asked for a more pleasant stay than my idyll in Orchha.

Sunset as seen from palace roof. Orchha.

Nineteenth century painting depicting mounted warriors who protected Orchha, the capital of a once powerful Rajput kingdom. Lakshmi Narayan Temple.

Ram Raja Temple was once a palace. It is said that it was turned into a temple when a temporarily installed image of Rama proved impossible to move, although today the statue is located elsewhere. 17th century.

Royal tombs (chhatris) on the bank of the Betwa River were memorials to Orchha's rulers. 17th - 18th century.

Khajuraho

After a five day visit to Orchha, I took a bus crowded with villagers to Khajuraho. Its splendid temples, which draw travelers from all over the world, are one of India's four most frequently visited attractions. Originally there were 85 ornate Hindu temples, though only 22 remain. Most of the medieval temples still standing date from 950 to 1050 A.D., which partially accounts for the site's architectural cohesiveness. In addition, the Vishnu and Shiva sects of Hinduism, as well as Jains who built there, all employed the same style. The six hour trip across the uninspiring, flat and dusty terrain was of little interest, and it definitely would be best to fly if coming from New Delhi, Agra or Banaras.

My bus arrived late in the evening and after checking into a hotel, I went in search of food. Though Khajuraho is a village of fewer than 10,000 people, it has a wide variety of places to eat. Because it was a pleasant night, I chose to dine at an outdoor restaurant, which was lighted only by candles. I ordered an all-you-can-eat vegetarian *thali*, which meant I would be served as much of the four vegetable preparations as I desired. The inexpensive meal was excellent and was one of the best values that I had in all of India. Any one of the single servings would have been worth the cost of the entire meal. I had requested that the proprietor use less spicy seasonings than he normally would, and to my delight, the meal was prepared perfectly to my taste. All the dishes were delicious, including the fried okra, which did make me a little homesick for southern American foods. Though *dhal* (lentils) is included in all basic fare, its thick sauce gave this staple legume a gourmet flair. I always enjoyed mixing yogurt with the *dhal* and used a *chapati* (thin, flat bread) to scoop it up. Although silverware was provided, using one's fingers is the accepted way to eat in most places in India. The owner evidently knew how to cook for Westerners. The *palak panir* (spinach with cubed, soft cheese) was not overcooked. A delicate combination of coriander and cumin turned what appeared to be the thinly sliced stalk of a very plain vegetable into a tasty curry, which I ate with *basmati* rice. The meal was so good that it took will power not to overeat.

Vishvanath Temple, Khajuraho. Chandella Dynasty, ca. 1002 A.D.

Khajuraho, Madhya Pradesh

Javari Temple silhouetted at sunset. Khajuraho. Chandella Dynasty, ca. 1075 - 1100 A.D.

The next morning I was eager to visit the temples at Khajuraho. I walked the quarter of a mile from my hotel, and as the temples came into view, I realized why there were so many visitors. The temple complex was carefully designed to create an attitude of reverence in the pilgrim from his very first glance. Each temple is impressively situated on a high stone platform. Because of the additional elevation, I had to raise my eyes upwards to view the entire structure, which made it seem even more grandiose. But it was the tall sandstone towers — so strikingly silhouetted against a bright blue sky — that immediately caught my attention. Although today's traveler sees these soaring towers in their weathered sandstone color, during the Medieval period when the temples were built, they were coated with white stucco to create the illusion of being snow covered peaks of the Himalayan mountains. Even without the white coating, I stood in awe of these graceful structures.

A Muslim historian in the eleventh century referred to Khajuraho as "the City of the Gods." It would seem to be a miracle that the city was not destroyed during the Muslim invasion of Hindustan when Delhi, Somnath and Mathura were sacked. Again in 1193, the iconoclastic armies of Islam marched into the heart of India. They destroyed many temples and towns, but Khajuraho, which had by then lost its political importance, was once more miraculously spared. This enabled the Chandella Dynasty to survive another 350 years.

One of the most artistic sculptures at Khajuraho is of an *apsara*, a heavenly nymph, removing a thorn from her foot. Other scenes, both human and divine, are to be found at the numerous temples. But it is the graceful, full-bosomed *apsaras* who make the stone carvings come alive. They are portrayed in over sixteen moods and poses — applying eye make-up, putting on and taking off anklets, holding a mirror, dancing, and other intimate gestures.

No one seems to be sure why the erotic figures were carved. It seems to me that the most carnal sculptures of Khajuraho probably represented the sexual excesses of another philosophy called Tantra. These Tantric practices were eventually cast out by the alienated worshipers and priests who considered them taboo.

Heavenly nymph removing a thorn from her foot. Vishvanath Temple. Chandella Dynasty, ca. 1002 A.D.

Heavenly nymph holding a mirror while applying a mark (bindi or tilik) at her spiritual eye. Khajuraho. Mahadeva Temple, Chandella Dynasty, early 11th century.

The shikhara (tower) of the Kandariya Mahadeo Temple rises to a height of 102 feet. Khajuraho. Chandella Dynasty, ca. 1025 - 1050 A.D.

The *shikhara* (tower) of the great Kandariya Mahadeo Temple rises to a height of 102 feet and dominates the entire landscape. Hundreds of figures were carved in vertical bands that seemed to be a natural part of the buttresses which supported the tower. It was a perfect integration of art and architecture. The clever design of the giant tower directed my gaze upwards, as successive levels culminated at the top. Its effect was that heaven and earth had merged, which was the purpose for the tower being built directly over the most sacred part of the structure. The inner sanctum, or "holy of holies," enshrined an image of Shiva, the deity to whom the temple was dedicated.

After spending the morning photographing, I rented a bicycle to visit some other temples located about a mile away. Shortly after leaving the bicycle shop, I saw a young girl of about eight who was walking by the side of the road, probably returning from school since she was carrying her book bag. She was wearing a sweater and skirt whose length covered her knees. A piece of fancy white lace sewn near the hem made the homemade garment seem special. When she approached a roadside Hindu shrine that had a bell suspended beyond her reach, she climbed upon a concrete post so that she could ring it.

While the bell has spiritual significance for most religions of the world, on a physical level a Hindu rings one to attract the attention of God, much the same as we ring a doorbell to let someone know that we are there. This little girl was spontaneously trying to get God's attention to express her devotion. Her gaze of concentration as she rang the bell indicated that she had "serious business" with the Lord. In a way, she was talking to Him saying, "Lord, here I am. Don't forget me."

I jumped off my bicycle and captured the event on film. Her sincere devotional outpouring of love for God touched my heart. While most travelers to Khajuraho remember it for the erotic stone carvings, my fondest memory is of this young girl ringing the bell by the roadside shrine.

Girl ringing bell at Hindu roadside shrine to attract God's attention. Khajuraho.

Upon reaching the village, I continued down a dirt road which led to an isolated temple in the middle of a cultivated field. Nearby, I observed a small boy tending two cows connected to a single yoke. The animals walked around a circular course at the urging of the boy's long stick and, no doubt, as a result of many years of habit. They provided the power to turn a wooden water wheel which scooped water from a deep well. As the water filled clay jugs on the upward cycle of the wheel's rotation, the downward turn emptied the precious liquid into a trench which joined another canal and finally transported the life giving stream into the fields. In the background was the temple, and I realized this could have been a scene from a thousand years ago. Except for the medieval sanctuary, little had changed here for 5,000 years. This was the magic of a visit to Khajuraho.

Boy prodding cows to turn water wheel. In the background is Vamana Temple. Khajuraho, ca. 11th century.

◁ *Opposite*
Priest performing Hatha Yoga posture in
front of statue of Hanuman, dating to
922 A.D. Khajuraho. Hanuman Temple.

Bhopal

My travels next took me to Bhopal, a city of over a million people. Today, Bhopal is known for the Union Carbide disaster, when poisonous gas escaped from a plant in December of 1984. The deadly chemical cloud killed over 4,000 people in the world's worst industrial disaster, but the real story of the present city is its Mughal history which dates back to 1707. As my bus came over a hill, it approached the outskirts of the city. One of India's largest mosques dominated the view.

Eager to get a closer look, I immediately went to the mosque and entered the walled courtyard through the massive main gate. The imposing three white domes over the main structure were reflected in a square pool of azure water located in the middle of the courtyard. The two minarets flanking the front of the building were so tall that I had to crane my neck backwards to see their tops.

Small groups of students were sitting around the courtyard. Older men were instructing them in the Koran. I could feel such strong undercurrents of peace as I stood there, it gave me hope that someday there will be harmony among all religions. I walked over to one of the scholars to learn some additional history about the mosque, and we began a friendly discourse. He said to me very proudly, "We are making a big investment in our future. We are teaching our youth to be human beings." Evidently they were succeeding, for several of the teenage Muslim boys who came over to meet me were models of politeness.

Muslim students studying the Koran. Taj-ul-Masjid, Bhopal.

Muslims praying at conclusion of Ramadan. Taj-ul-Masjid, Bhopal.

An estimated 10,000 worshipers bow facing Mecca during a holiday celebrating the conclusion of Ramadan. Taj-ul-Masjid (mosque), Bhopal.

Several years later, at that same mosque in Bhopal, I had the good fortune to attend the holiday celebrating the end of Ramadan. For an entire month, Muslims observe a daily fast from dawn until sunset. The courtyard was jammed. I was the only Westerner there and possibly the only non-Muslim out of perhaps 10,000 worshipers gathered. I noticed that all of the males were wearing the traditional round Muslim cap, a *kufi*. I went to the mosque's office and asked if I should cover my head or wear a cap. The administrator broke into a big smile as he replied, "Just pray with your head uncovered." Though I was unfamiliar with the Muslim ritual of how and when to bow, no one seemed to mind. Afterwards, several Muslims greeted me cordially, and I was glad I had participated in the prayers.

Sanchi

I was eager to get to the famous Buddhist site at Sanchi. While looking out the window on the bus during the hour and a half journey, I saw an old man digging with a pickax by the side of the road. As he labored, he also attended a baby sleeping peacefully in a rope cradle which was tied between a fence and a telephone pole. As our bus continued towards Sanchi, we passed a large group of village women who were swinging heavy pickaxes and transporting broken stones in large containers skillfully balanced on their heads. They were dressed in colorful saris and wearing an abundance of silver jewelry. I was surprised at how finely dressed the women were while doing their menial jobs, and how clean they managed to keep themselves. At one of the local stops, a young peasant woman boarded with four children. They were on the bus for over an hour, and their cheerfulness while standing in the crowded aisle was amazing. The oldest girl, about 10 years old, often held her baby sister, to give her mother a rest. She cradled her so lovingly that the baby was as content with her sister as she was in her mother's arms. Because I was tired myself, I all the more appreciated that these children had learned to behave, regardless of external circumstances.

On a hill rising from the wide plain of Central India stand some of the oldest Buddhist structures in that country. Architecturally and artistically, Sanchi is India's most impressive Buddhist site. The dome of the Great Stupa (shrine) was embellished with an outer covering of brick-like stone added at the end of the first century B.C. It is believed to be the first use of stone masonry on an architectural building in India.

The shape of the simple domed *stupa* dates back more than 2,200 years with its architectural origins stemming from primitive stone-covered earthen burial mounds. As Buddhism spread throughout Asia, the *stupa's* simple shape evolved into different forms: the pagodas of Burma and China, the *chorten* of Tibet, and the "world mountain" of Borobudur in Central Java, considered by art historians to be the greatest of all Buddhist *stupas*.

The Great Stupa of Sanchi does not directly connect to the events of the Buddha's life. It did not become an important religious center until approximately 200 years after it was built by the great Mauryan Emperor Ashoka, who made Buddhism the official state religion in 255 B.C. He began a vigorous building project which continued for almost 1,000 years until the crest of the sacred hill was covered with *stupas, viharas* (monasteries) and temples. Though most of the ancient buildings are today in ruins, the Greek style portico of a Gupta Dynasty temple dating back to 5th century A.D. reminded me of an acropolis in Greece.

With the gradual decline of Buddhism after the 7th century A.D., the hill was slowly abandoned and eventually forgotten as it was covered by dense vegetation. Ironically, its jungle canopy spared the Buddhist sanctuaries from the usual destruction by later Islamic invasions. It was discovered in 1818 by a British officer. Formal restoration began in 1881 and it was completed in the early 20th century.

Detail of gate. Great Stupa, Sanchi. Andhra Dynasty, late 1st century B.C. - early 1st century A.D.

The Great Stupa (shrine) of Sanchi, as viewed from the east. Shunga and early Andhra Dynasties, 3rd century B.C. - early 1st century A.D. Height of gate is 34 feet.
◁ *Left and opposite* ▷

Inner face of western gate (torana) at Sanchi. Scenes from the life of the Buddha, winged lions, the stupa and the wheel. Andhra Dynasty, late 1st century B.C. - early 1st century A.D. Sandstone.

It is the Great Stupa with its four magnificently carved gates, 34 feet high, that make the site famous. Two of the four gates which mark the entrances withstood an earthquake and have been standing for over 2,000 years. Depicted on the square columns of the gates and their elegant, triple cross-members are episodes from the life of the Buddha and his previous incarnations. I considered the four gates to the Great Stupa among the most impressive artistic masterpieces that I saw in India.

From the top of the hill, I had a panoramic view of the green plains below. For Buddhists, the ascent merely begins their pilgrimage. Immediately upon passing through the gates, the supplicants are drawn into a prescribed circular pathway to be followed in a clockwise direction. Depending on their devotion, they prayerfully circumnavigate the *stupa* three, seven, or for the most pious, 108 times. Then, the pilgrims climb stairs onto the roof of the shrine, a symbol of the Buddha's transcendental state of *nirvana*. Bolstered by the knowledge that a relic of the great sage was contained in the structure beneath them, the devotees strive to achieve sacred harmony with the higher world.

The physically taxing bus trip to get to this remote site was certainly worth the inconvenience. Because of my love for religious art and architecture, standing in front of the Great Stupa was like being a pilgrim myself.

Young girls in front of a Hindu temple, holding prashad (divinely blessed sweets) which they received inside. Ujjain.

Ujjain

Located in the western part of the state, Ujjain is connected by several major rail routes which made it easy for me to reach. After so many bus trips, the comfort of traveling by train was a joy. The camaraderie within the compartment of a coach often becomes an event itself. Having sufficient food to eat was never a problem. Indian travelers frequently pack picnic meals which they often shared with me. Express trains offered inexpensive, adequate hot meals, or I could buy from the vendors who passed up and down the aisles. When the train stopped at major stations, the platforms were filled with small stands and rolling carts where a variety of hot foods, fruits, vegetables and drinks could be purchased. I always brought a liter of bottled water with me as it was unwise for me to drink the local water. Someone within my compartment usually spoke English, and by the end of the trip, we often exchanged addresses.

On this particular journey, I departed the train in Ujjain to do some sightseeing, though my ultimate destination that day was about 50 miles away in Indore. Ujjain is an ancient and holy city to the Hindus. It is located on the right bank of the Shipra River, and has numerous temples situated along its banks. There are many bathing *ghats*, whose steps lead down to the river to facilitate pilgrims' ritual bathing. Ujjain is one of the four sacred cities which hosts a huge religious festival drawing millions of pilgrims. The event, the *Kumbha Mela*, which lasts about a month and takes place every three years, rotates consecutively among Allahabad (85 miles west of Banaras), Nasik (115 miles northeast of Bombay), Ujjain (420 miles southwest of Agra) and Hardwar (located 138 miles northeast of Delhi on the Ganges River in the Himalayan foothills). These sites were chosen by fate as gods and demons quarreled in heaven over an elixir which promised immortality to the one who would drink it. As they fought, a drop fell on each of these four fortunate cities.

I hired a bicycle rickshaw to take me to Mahakaleshwar Temple, since I had some time before the departure of a city tour I would be taking. When we neared the temple, I suddenly became aware of a sweet fragrance permeating the air. It wafted by like a gentle breeze as we passed a row of simple wooden flower stalls. Large garlands of pink, orange and white blossoms were suspended in front of the shops and created a wall of flowers in the midst of this modest, provincial city.

In India, devotion is often expressed and represented by flowers. Usually a worshiper would not go to a temple without taking an offering. I selected a pink lotus, an ancient symbol in India, because its unfolding petals represent the expansion of the soul. Its purity and loveliness blossom from the mud of its origin, forecasting a spiritual transformation for all.

Flower stalls. Ujjain.

Family praying before abstract image, symbolizing God beyond creation who cannot be put into form. Ujjain.

Hindu priest pouring wine into the mouth of a shrine figure of Kal Bhairava. Painted stone, cloth and flowers. Ujjain.

Jyotirlingam, representing the Holy Spirit's presence in the universe. Mahakaleshwar Temple. Ujjain.

Mahakaleshwar Temple, dedicated to Lord Shiva, was destroyed in 1235 but since has been restored. The tall spire made it appropriately impressive to house one of India's 12 sacred Shiva shrines known as *Jyotirlinga*, which were believed to have self-created themselves through the power of a *mantra*. The sacred stone Shiva *lingam*, a phallic symbol of the Holy Spirit's creative power, was placed in the center of a small shrine room in the basement and was covered with garlands. A low wall prevented the pilgrims from directly approaching the *lingam*, but it could be touched with an outstretched hand. Because there were at least three times more people present than the space could comfortably accommodate, I had to wait several minutes before I could enter and approach the sacred object. Observing the worshipers was engrossing. If the reader can imagine the Holy Spirit residing in a stone, the pushing and shoving that would transpire to get close to it, and the adoration that would ensue, then possibly the reader would know what it was like to be there. A priest received flower offerings from the pilgrims and gave them *prashad*, ritually blessed sweets, in return. The devotion of those present had a profound impact on me.

As visually exciting as the shrine room was at Mahakaleshwar Temple, I was not prepared for the symbolic ritual which occurred at a small riverside temple, where followers of Shiva worship the eight Bhairavs. Chief among those divine companions is Kal Bhairava, to whom the temple was dedicated. A priest appeared who was dressed in white. In one hand he clutched a clear glass bottle filled with red wine. In the other, he held a shallow metal bowl. Pouring wine into the vessel, he then placed it against the lips of the shrine figure. Tilting his wrist upwards, he poured the liquid into the heavenly being's mouth, and for all practical purposes, it appeared that the image drank the wine. It was the most unusual ritual I saw in all of India, particularly since wine is rarely used as a sacrament in Hindu temples.

Shrine figure underneath banyan tree on bank of Shipra River. Painted stone and flowers. Ujjain.

Immediately behind the temple on the banks of the Shipra was a large banyan tree. Its trunk and many vines which had dropped to the ground from its branches had been painted reddish orange. Much of the paint had faded and peeled, giving the tree the effect of being an object which had been ritually encrusted with pigment. It was a perfect setting for an unconventional shrine. This banyan tree had been invested with the same religious sanctity as other well-known holy trees which are found throughout India. Underneath the tree was an image, and when I saw it I was stunned by its similarity to a New Guinea (Gulf of Papua) gable mask. It was about three feet high and consisted only of an elongated head and neck. It, too, had been ritually painted with many coats of reddish orange pigment, making it impossible for me to ascertain what the material was. I would have liked to have spent more time there, but the bus conductor of my tour blew his whistle which indicated it was time to go.

Indore

When the tour was completed, I walked the short distance to the bus station. I was going to Indore where I would be staying with a friend whom I had met in Ahmedabad, where we both were guests in the same home. It was 6:00 p.m., the bus was crammed with people, and there was not a single inch of room for another passenger. Traveling on an Indian train or bus with baggage at rush hour is unwise — or perhaps insane — and is best avoided.

The 50 mile trip took almost two hours. When I arrived, my host's wife prepared warm water for me on a gas burner so I could bathe. My host, who was about 50, was an attorney, and used the front room of his two story home for an office. They had two children, a son who was studying for his high school diploma exams and a daughter who was fifteen. I had mailed them a postcard that I was coming, and they had been waiting for me since that afternoon. Their son "Bunti" addressed me as "Uncle," and I grew to like the appellation and its significance.

That night my host told me about a pilgrimage he and his wife had made to Jammu in the Himalayan Mountains of northwestern India. The elevation was approximately 18,000 feet and required considerable physical exertion since it was a several days' climb and was completely by foot. His facial expression softened as he reminisced about how peaceful it was meditating there on the banks of a glacier fed river. His wife confided that she had felt so "satisfied" inwardly in that spiritual environment that she thought seriously of not returning — a remarkable statement for a woman who was totally dedicated to serving her family. A physical malady made it difficult for her to walk. Just making the trip required tremendous determination and devotion. Accounts such as these increased my admiration for the Indian tradition to seek God.

Lord Shiva, King of Yogis, garlanded with marigolds and seated in the lotus position. The mosaic decoration of the shrine is made from small pieces of colored glass. Hindu temple, Indore.

Holy island of Omkareshwar. Home to one of India's twelve most sacred Shiva temples, it is also the location where Shankara, India's most illustrious philosopher, met his guru.

Omkareshwar

Early the following morning Bunti took me to the bus station. Before my departing, his mother had prepared a big breakfast to fortify me for the all day journey to an important pilgrimage site 60 miles away. The meal began with a bowl of seasonal fruit which included bananas and mangoes. Several of the varieties were indigenous to the region but were unfamiliar to me. I grew very fond of one of these exotic fruits, which had a brown skin and looked like a kiwi but tasted considerably sweeter. Several of the hardy dishes she served such as cornbread with a thick chickpea curry over it were so filling that to me the meal seemed like lunch.

When we arrived at the terminal, Bunti showed me to my bus. He went aboard with me and found a passenger who would make sure that I took the correct bus when we transferred en route.

The bus ride was much like the others. The windows were jarred open by the bumpy road, which resulted in the early hours of travel being uncomfortably cold. I was glad that I had worn a warm jacket. The faulty suspension system of the old vehicle was no match for the road's deep potholes, and I knew that we were in for a rough ride.

We were dropped off at the bus station on the outskirts of the small town of Omkareshwar. The town was built on the banks of the sacred river Narmada. Two of India's 12 great Shiva temples were said to have been located on the island in the middle of the river. My purpose for coming here was to pay homage to the memory of one of the wisest minds the world has ever known. The thought of walking in his footprints thrilled me. His name was Shankara. Though many Indian historians rank him as one of the 12 greatest persons who ever lived, India's most illustrious philosopher is little known in the United States and not even mentioned in American encyclopedias. Nonetheless, his impact on world thought is profound.

Though Western scholars do not agree on the century of his birth, Indians believe he was born to Brahmin parents circa 788 A.D. in a small village of Western Malabar in Southern India. By the age of 10 he was an academic prodigy, having read and memorized all of the scriptures. He also had written commentaries on many of them, and famous scholars from all parts of the country came to seek his scriptural interpretations. His father died when Shankara was a young boy. He persuaded his mother to allow him to renounce the world, and he took the monastic vows of poverty, chastity and obedience.

It was on the banks of the river Narmada at Omkareshwar that Shankara met a famous philosopher and seer, Gaudapada, who had attained oneness with the Divine. The young boy asked the old man to initiate him, but instead he sent the lad to his foremost disciple, Govinda Jati, who accepted him as his disciple and instructed him in meditation and the entire process of yoga. In a surprisingly short time, Shankara achieved complete self-realization, the union of soul with Spirit.

During Shankara's lifetime, India was passing through a period of spiritual decadence. Hinduism was on the wane, having been encumbered by priestly dogma. Buddhism, too, was in a state of decline. Many Buddhists misunderstood what was required of them if they were to attain the transcendental state of *nirvana*. They thought to reach the "void" of *nirvana* meant total annihilation of the self. But the Buddha was referring to the ego, the "little self," which first must be overcome before the higher Self can attain liberation. It was during this era of spiritual confusion that Shankara brought timely reform to Hinduism. Redefining the goal of life as being one with the ever-existing, ever-conscious, ever-new bliss of Spirit, he taught a positive interpretation of God that was very much needed in the world. Not surprisingly, many followers of Buddhism turned to his teachings, and millions came to listen to the practical wisdom of the barefooted young monk.

Man standing on rocky bluff overlooking Narmada River, drying recently dyed cloth. Omkareshwar.

Boat ferrying pilgrims across Narmada River. Omkareshwar.

Shankara was a rare combination of saint, scholar and teacher. In his brief 32 year life span, he visited every part of India, spending many years in arduous travel. He established *maths*, monastic education centers, in the four corners of India to promote religious and national unity. These influential centers still exist and are located in Mysore in the south, Puri in the east, Dwarka in the west, and Badrinath in the Himalayan north.

Having mastered yoga, Shankara had developed extraordinary powers that many Westerners attribute only to Jesus. A mental feat credited to him concerned his disciple Sanandana, who wrote a commentary on the philosophy of the <u>Brahma Sutras</u>. The manuscript was destroyed by fire, but Shankara, who had only once glanced through it, repeated it word for word to the author. The text, known as the <u>Panchapadika</u>, is still studied by scholars.

When seated on a river bank one day, his disciple Sanandana heard Shankara calling him from the opposite shore. As he faithfully entered the swirling current to go to his guru, his feet were supported by a series of lotus flowers which Shankara materialized on top of the water. Sanandana was thereafter known as Padmapada ("lotus-foot"). Even more spectacular, after his beloved mother died, Shankara cremated her body with heavenly fire that spurted forth from his upraised hands.

As the morning light began to burn away the mist that hovered about this ancient village, I thought of the power of clarity Shankara had given not only to the Indians of that time, but also to the many generations that followed. I walked the well-worn path into the small town of Omkareshwar, passing numerous stalls which sold religious objects. In front of one, mounds of brightly colored powders used for cosmetics and religious markings were placed side by side on round trays. The heaps of purple, lavender, vermilion and ochre powders looked like a palette for a cosmic artist. Behind the cosmetics, small religious pictures were placed neatly on low tiered shelves. Hanging above them were two rows of beads. A young boy stood on the edge of the table.

Following the other pilgrims, we passed over a small hill, where I got my first look at the sacred island. I was exhilarated. I had no preconceived image of what Omkareshwar would look like, and I had not expected such an ethereal landscape. The large island consisted of a steep, rocky hill whose prominent landmark was the massive tower of a Shiva temple. The buildings and temples were constructed in medieval Hindu architectural style, which emphasized the protective nature of walled fortresses of that era. The scene looked like a 17th century classical painting by the French artist Nicolas Poussin. A haze blurred the scene, giving the appearance that the island rose from the river. This view could have been Poussin's sought-after fantasy.

Sikh shopkeeper. Omkareshwar.

Stall which sells mementos to pilgrims. Colored powders are used for cosmetics and as religious markings by various sects. Omkareshwar.

◁ *Opposite*
Women selling flowers on steps leading to Omkareshwar's famous Shiva temple.

Ascetic (sadhu) holding Shiva trident. Omkareshwar.

Hindu folk art shrine (note brown stone Shiva lingam with gold ritual markings in left foreground). Omkareshwar.

It was as if I were standing in the painting's foreground on clearly definable soil. Separating me from this holy island was the blue-green water of a river perhaps 40 yards wide. On the other side was the longed for paradise of Arcadia, which always seemed to be illusive and just over the next horizon. Through God's grace, I had found my Arcadia.

I crossed the old stone bridge which spanned the river. As I reached the other side, I enjoyed walking along the narrow lanes. After visiting the famous 1,200 year old Shiva temple, I hired a small boat to row me upstream so I could swim at a sacred spot in the river. The ruins of many temples destroyed by time and the invading Muslims lined both its banks. After a refreshing swim, I ate the picnic lunch my hostess had prepared for me. Feeling very content, I was grateful to have made my pilgrimage to this pastoral location where Shankara had attained his enlightenment.

My visit to Omkareshwar was one of the great unexpected pleasures of my trip to India. I had never heard of it until my host from Indore suggested that I go there. I felt that the invisible hand of destiny was again guiding my life.

I returned to Indore in time for the evening meal. After dinner my host recited a few Sanskrit prayers so I could hear the euphony of the language. On several occasions he evidently made mistakes, because his wife and daughter would laughingly correct him as if he were a schoolboy who had made an error in his recitation. Though they did it good-naturedly, at that moment his role as head of the family was unapparent as he meekly smiled in embarrassment. Later, when we were alone, my host confided to me that I meant a lot to him, and that if I ever needed to, I could come live with his family.

One evening, when he asked me how many sisters I had, I replied, "None." The word was scarcely out of my mouth when his daughter Gudia, with whom I had become quite close, emphatically said, "One!" Her reply reminded me of my visit with a family in Ahmedabad in the state of Gujarat. When I referred to myself as "Uncle," my host's daughter immediately said, "Brother." And when her brother said to me, "We think of you often," she blurted out, "Always!" Such spontaneous outpourings of love and devotion deeply touched my heart.

Gwalior

My trip to Gwalior made a lasting impression because of my visit to the tomb of a Muslim Sufi saint. I spotted the structure's large roof from the ramparts of Gwalior Fort and was curious to see what the edifice might be. Upon arriving at the site, I learned that the saint's name was Mohammed Ghaus, who had lived during the 16th century. For some reason, which is still unknown to me, he also was held in reverence by Hindus. When I entered the shrine, I was surprised to see that Hindus and Muslims were worshiping there together. Considering the long history of antagonisms which have existed between followers of the two religions, this was a remarkable sight.

Though turmoil often exists in India between different factions, her religious communities have lived harmoniously in spite of some zealots' selfish motives. Because of the tolerance of Hinduism, I believe that eventually India will become the example for global ecumenicism, showing today's multicultural world that peace is possible amongst diverse populations. I witnessed Hindus and Muslims sharing the same shrine in Gwalior, Hindus and Buddhists worshiping at the same religious site in Darjeeling, and Hindus and Christians praying together at the Church of our Lady of Good Health in Velakanni in South India. Even Guru Nanak, the founder of the Sikh religion, is revered by Hindus and Muslims as well as Sikhs. If different religious communities can worship together in parts of India, surely the rest of India and the world can do the same.

The tomb of Mohammed Ghaus, built in 1564. The Muslim Sufi saint is revered by Muslims and Hindus and both worship there. Prayer requests are posted on tomb. Gwalior.

Gwalior, Madhya Pradesh

Gwalior is famous for its large old fort, built atop a hill which rises over 100 yards above the old town and dominates the surrounding countryside. During the fort's 1,000 year history, it changed hands many times, including twice to the British. As I walked up the long ascent, turrets topped by domed cupolas, serving as ominous sentinels, reminded me of the many invaders who must have paid with their lives trying to conquer it.

Gwalior is located on the Delhi to Bombay rail line, yet few Westerners ever go there, missing some of the most interesting medieval Jain sculptures in all of India. The mammoth carved figures were cut into the cliffs during the mid-1400s and are located on the many approaches to the fort. The bold relief carvings of these Jain saints were defaced by invading Muslim forces in 1527, but since have been restored.

*Large sculptures of Jain Tirthankaras (saints) carved into the
cliffs on the approaches to Gwalior Fort. Mid-1400s.*

17th century Gwalior Fort dominates the surrounding countryside.

My journeys in Central India to Omkareshwar, Sanchi and the mosque in Bhopal were inspiring and the memories endearing. Though Omkareshwar is Hindu, the *stupa* at Sanchi, Buddhist, and Bhopal's Taj-ul-Masjid, Muslim — God's peaceful vibration makes no distinction for religious and cultural differences.

Chapter Two

The East

Bodhi Tree, historical location of Buddha's enlightenment and the most sacred Buddhist pilgrimage site in the world. Bodh Gaya, Bihar.

Buddha seated in meditation, "Calling the Earth to Witness" his triumph over delusion. Stone and cloth. Bodh Gaya.

West Bengal, Sikkim, Orissa and Bihar

The scenery and cultural diversity of the four states included in this region are striking. Spectacular snow-topped Himalayan Mountain ranges surround West Bengal's Darjeeling and the neighboring Indian state of Sikkim. Further south, the landscape quickly flattens into the basin of the Ganges. Continuing eastward, the mighty Ganges River flows onward to the coast, where its tributaries form countless estuaries and its sacred water finally empties into the Bay of Bengal. About 35 miles from the coast, the sprawling city of Calcutta is located on the east bank of the Hooghly River, a tributary of the Ganges.

Orissa, the state south of Bengal on India's eastern seaboard, is tropical and has sandy beaches which stretch for miles. Conveniently located close to one another are three important temple towns: Bhubaneswar with its hundreds of Orissan style temples, many over 1,000 years old; Konarak, renown for its Sun Temple; and Puri, home to one of India's most famous religious festivals known for its giant floats which require thousands of men to pull them. Once each year during June or July the revered image of Lord Jagannath, an incarnation of Vishnu as Lord of the Universe, is removed from Puri's most sacred Jagannath Temple. It is placed upon a huge "temple car." Hundreds of thousands of pilgrims and tourists line the parade route to see the incredible floats, the largest of which is over 42 feet high.

To the west is the state of Bihar, where I traced the footsteps of Buddha to Bodh Gaya, the historical location where he became enlightened while meditating under a Banyan tree.

Most of the mountainous northeastern area of India, located east of Sikkim, is home to various ethnic groups. Many of these areas are off limits to foreigners to protect and preserve indigenous tribal cultures so I shall not include that region in this book.

Calcutta: The Pulse of Bengal

From New Delhi, I took an overnight express train to Calcutta. When the train stopped at major stations, the piercing shouts of vendors and noisy passengers and well-wishers caused me to yearn for the peace of the countryside. As the train departed, the rhythmic clacking of the wheels on the rails was a welcomed and soothing sound. Watching scenes flash by outside the window added to the mesmerizing effect.

The train arrived early the next morning in Calcutta. Howrah Station was already teeming with people. Over a million travelers, hawkers and porters use this massive Victorian terminal each day. Indian Railways is the world's largest employer with over 1.6 million people. It is estimated that 80 million persons depend on it for a livelihood. It still uses perhaps 6,000 steam locomotives to transport more than nine million passengers a day. With over 37,000 miles of track, it is the fourth longest route system in the world. The dust and soot that blows through the open windows cover the passengers and make it difficult to stay clean. Thank goodness there is a good, inexpensive, one day laundry service at most hotels.

I made my way through the crowds to the sidewalk, where I stood in a "queue" to wait for a metered taxi. For those in a hurry, an abundance of unmetered taxis are available, and drivers charge whatever the market will bear. I hired a taxi to take me to the *ashram*, or monastery, where I would be staying. It was located about 12 miles north of Calcutta, which has a dense population of over 11 million. Upon leaving the station, we immediately crossed over the 450 meter long Howrah Bridge. This cantilevered bridge, which spans the Hoogley without any pylons in the river, is the busiest bridge in the world. Looking through my taxi's window I observed the pedestrians' faces, where timeless adversity had etched its unmistakable lines.

I was glad when we arrived at the *ashram* which offered seclusion from contact with so many people. It was built on the bank of the Hoogley in the suburb of Dakshineswar. The driver blew his horn and someone opened the gate for us to enter. Once inside, I heard sacred music coming from across the river, and I tingled with delight. The peacefulness of the *ashram* enabled me to put others' misfortunes out of my mind for the present.

The guest rooms and meals were basic. The "mattress" was so thin that I had to place some clothes between it and the hard wooden bed frame just to be able to sleep. Although the bed had mosquito netting, I made the mistake of not using it and was awakened sometime after midnight as swarms of mosquitoes attacked me in a "feeding frenzy." I arranged the mosquito netting around the bed as quickly as possible, and finally went back to sleep.

I awoke early the next morning to the exotic sounds of birds. I associated their calls with the jungles of South America. Their strange warbling created a counterpoint to the drone of a nearby ferry's outboard motor. It was only six a.m. and Calcutta already was offering me an overture to the day's grand performance.

I spent the morning and early afternoon in the solitude of the *ashram* grounds. Its peaceful environment was the perfect prescription for a tattered traveler whose nerves had become frayed from a frenetic itinerary. During a conversation with one of the monks, I mentioned that an American friend had given me 500 dollars to distribute among the poor. He replied that they would be happy to have 100 dollars for a leper colony that they served, and suggested that I give the rest to Mother Teresa's mission for the poor and homeless. I was touched by his unselfishness.

Early the following morning, I walked to the nearby Kali Temple, which was built in 1847.

Kali Temple. Dakshineswar/Calcutta.
Built in 1847.

◁ *Opposite*
Built in the mid-19th century, St. Paul's Cathedral is
a reminder of British Calcutta. Sunrise.

Flower stalls located near Kali Temple. Dakshineswar/ Calcutta.

Devotees waiting to enter Kali Temple. Dakshineswar/ Calcutta.

Kali Temple has become famous in more recent years due to its connection with the God-illumined yogi and philosopher, Sri Ramakrishna, who preached the unity of all religions. Although the temple did not open until 6 a.m., many pilgrims were already there. The men and women formed separate lines and entered from opposite sides. I noticed that most of them were carrying flowers for an offering, many of which were deep red hibiscus, the color associated with Kali. Like the others, I was eager to see the black stone statue of Kali, which was said to have taken a human form in honor of Ramakrishna who once served there as a priest.

The female figure of Kali represents God in the aspect of eternal Mother Nature. The black, four-armed woman is standing on the recumbent white form of the God Shiva, who represents the Infinite from which all activities of Nature originate. Her four arms symbolize two beneficent and two destructive attributes of the essential duality inherent in all creation. Wearing a garland of skulls, Kali can be awesome in her destructive role, as she annihilates all things back into the One, only to create again. In her function as Goddess of Destruction, she holds a severed head. Making inferences through the intellect, many assume that her sword is used only for human destruction. But it also is a symbol of her eternal vigil as she keeps guard over creation's planetary rhythms and balances. The message is that one should not seek absolute values in the relative world of nature, which is both benign and ruthless. The riddle of good and evil has been challenging humankind's minds since the beginning of recorded history.

After lunch at the *ashram*, I went to the nearby town of Serampore to visit a meditation *mandir* (temple) built to honor Sri Yukteswar, a yogic master of the 19th century. With incomparable discerning wisdom, his book The Holy Science documents the essential unity of Hinduism and Christianity.

That afternoon on the bus returning to the *ashram*, the conductor gently tapped me on the shoulder and indicated that I should move. To my embarrassment, I had been standing on the women's side of the bus! That was the only area outside of South India where I encountered separate seating sections on public buses for men and women.

I believe that separating the sexes in certain situations engenders respect for women. Over 40 years ago, an Indian master said that coeducation in the West had been a great failure because it had failed to teach moral principles. Considering the moral degeneration that has subsequently transpired, I wonder what he would have said today!

About 50 miles from Calcutta is the famous Shiva Temple of Tarakeswar. Because of the many spectacular healings which have taken place there, Hindus regard it with the same veneration that Catholics have for Lourdes in France. Because of its reputation, I was eager to go there. The two hour trip to Tarakeswar required that I first get across the Hooghley. The ferry was an open boat perhaps 15 feet long. The outboard motor was so old that flowers had been reverently placed on it in hopes that it would last another day. Due to the strong current of the Hooghley, the navigator had to aim the overcrowded craft upstream from our destination. The fare was three cents.

Once on the other side, I took a bicycle rickshaw to the railroad station, where I boarded a local train. At each of the many stops, more and more pilgrims crowded aboard. I did not have to ask anyone to tell me when we arrived at Tarakeswar because at that stop almost everyone departed. I followed the hundreds of pilgrims through narrow winding lanes. Like other pilgrimage centers I had visited in India, both sides of the street were lined with stalls selling icons and religious mementos. At lunchtime I looked for a place where I could get something to eat. Though there were many stalls with large pots of hot food, I could not find a restaurant which met my standards for hygiene; thus, I bought my lunch from a vendor on the street who sold tasty morsels of chickpeas served on a washed leaf for a penny each.

On the way to the temple, I passed a yogi with his head buried in the ground. Evidently he could control at will the flow of his breath and the functioning of his internal organs. While it seemed a strange way to demonstrate *pranayama*, the control of life force in the body, I was impressed with his accomplishment. The coins in his offering plate indicated that poor Indian pilgrims were also appreciative.

Witnessing such a phenomenal event was astounding. Many Westerners even refuse to consider that it is possible to live without breathing. From my study of yoga, I understood exactly what I was seeing. The only thing I could not comprehend was why scientists have not investigated the yogic mastery of control over the breath. Combined with its accompanying transcendental mental states, I believe that the control of life force is one of the more important concepts ever conceived by the human mind.

When I entered the sacred Tarakeswar shrine, I saw that the altar consisted of only a round stone. Without marked beginning or end, it was an appropriate symbol of the Infinite. As I bowed in reverence to it, I was pushed from the rear by overly zealous pilgrims. I was knocked head-over-heels and landed on my back in mud saturated with libations. The stains on my white clothing permanently "marked" the occasion. I arrived back at the *ashram* just in time for the 5:00 p.m. meditation. It had been a most interesting day.

Yogi with head buried in the ground, demonstrating his mastery over control of the body's "life force." Tarakeswar, West Bengal.

Calcutta, West Bengal

I was invited one evening to chant with the young male employees of the *ashram* at a small temple overlooking the Hooghly. Because it could not hold everyone, I sat outside on the steps. Their devotion more than compensated for the cacophony of their loud, untrained voices.

The next day while having my camera bag repaired in the little town near the *ashram*, the artisan and I became instant friends. While I was talking to him, three children approached, who wanted to meet me. They were adorable. The proprietor taught me a few Bengali words which enabled me to greet them, and between smiles and giggles, we enjoyed each other's company. After departing, the older of the two girls came back. She carefully removed a small bundle from her dress pocket, which contained a large leaf. As she unwrapped it, I realized that inside were sweets which she had received from the priest at the temple across the street. Wanting to share her blessing with me, she pinched off a small piece of the cake and placed it in my hand. Although I was fasting that day, I ate the tidbit because it was *prashad*. The little girl looked at me and smiled and then went happily on her way. Such devotional unselfish acts are among my fondest memories of India.

The artisan from the luggage shop took me to a store to assist me in making a needed purchase. The proprietor wanted to order food for us, but my friend told him I was fasting. When the shopkeeper asked me why I "starved the body," I replied that since he was a Hindu, he would understand that we live by *prana*, cosmic vibratory energy, and were not sustained merely by food ("Man shall not live by bread alone"). I added, "Even though I am an American, I know that!" He laughed heartily in agreement. What a pleasure it was to be in a country whose people are the most metaphysically inclined in the world. For every word in the English language with a philosophical meaning, there are four corresponding words in Greek and 40 in Sanskrit. Almost any Hindu commentary on its scriptures will impress the reader with its deep spiritual insight.

My Indian friend, Shymal, invited me to have lunch with him that weekend. He, his wife and two children lived in a one room home. Though they were very poor materially, his wife's inner radiance belied their condition. She prepared a nice meal for us outside on a gas burner. After lunch, my host took me to the home of one of his neighbors. While there, I admired some crafts. As we were preparing to leave, the young artist offered to give me a large porcelain vase, but I explained that I could not accept it as it would get broken. She then brought me a small bouquet of artificial roses. I told her that I would use them for my daily meditation in front of my travel altar. Leaving the room abruptly, she returned with a bottle of perfume. She sprayed the artificial flowers so they would smell good for God. I still use the flowers at home on my altar. Though their fragrance has long faded, the memory of her simple gesture is perennially present.

Shymal and I made arrangements to meet again at his shop several days later. Usually, when I had an engagement with an Indian, I specified that the appointed time was G.M.T., Greenwich Mean Time, and not I.S.T., Indian Stretchable Time. I suspected that our rendezvous would be on an I.S.T. basis.

When I arrived, the shop was closed so I sat on a wall across the street. Two men were digging a hole in the dirt lane. As they sank deeper and deeper into the earth, I became aware of my friend's tardiness. Finally he appeared.

I had planned my arrival in Calcutta to coincide with the Durga Festival, the most popular Indian holiday. It is celebrated throughout all of India, although its name varies regionally. Durga is one of the major goddesses symbolizing the feminine form of creation, and is a consort of the god Shiva.

In West Bengal, elaborate images of Durga are made and placed in shrines which are specially built for the occasion. Some of the more impressive edifices, which are constructed by placing tightly stretched canvas over bamboo scaffolding, appear from a distance to be large temples. At the end of the holiday, the images of Durga are ceremonially immersed into the sacred Hooghly River and the shrines are taken down.

Opposite ▷
Durga image being immersed in Hooghly River at conclusion of Durga Festival. Calcutta.

Calcutta, West Bengal

One evening, just before the festival was over, I asked Shymal to hire a taxi for us. Together with his family, we spent the remainder of that night and the next morning visiting as many of the Durga shrines in Calcutta as time permitted. We all had a wonderful time. It was like attending a Mardi Gras that still had religious significance. Often, when we neared the more elaborate shrines, the roads were so crowded with people that we had to vacate our taxi and make arrangements to meet the driver later.

It is the custom for Bengalis to purchase new clothing for the festival as a respectful gesture to God. I noticed that many of the poorer families appeared to have on new clothing, which was apparently homemade.

On a subsequent trip to India, my friend Shymal asked me to accompany him and his family to his mother's village, located less than 100 miles north of Calcutta near the border of Bangladesh. Naturally, I was thrilled with the opportunity and immediately accepted.

Durga image made in contemporary style. Durga Festival, Calcutta.

Durga traditional iconography. Durga Festival, Bagh Bazaar. Calcutta.

Opposite ▷
Women waiting to enter Kalighat Temple. Those in foreground with red powdered faces have already been consecrated by a priest. Juice from green coconuts is a popular drink. Durga Festival, Calcutta.

Village of Saula, West Bengal

We left by train for his village a few days later. When we arrived, Shymal hired a bicycle rickshaw to take our luggage and his children to his mother's home, while he, his wife and I walked. We stopped in the small town at a sweets shop, where I bought an assortment of delicious looking cookies as a gift for his mother.

Before entering her home, Shymal and his wife knelt respectfully at his mother's feet, which is the custom. When I did the same, she seemed pleased, and placed her hands upon my head as if blessing me. Though she did not speak English, there was an immediate rapport between us. She lived in a simple house like one might expect to see anywhere in the tropics. There was also a small separate structure that served as a kitchen. She insisted that I sleep in the main bedroom, but I refused, knowing that either she or her son and his wife would have to sleep on the floor of the other small bedroom. I found a storeroom attached to the front of the house and insisted that I stay there. When they saw that I was serious, the space was cleaned and prepared for me. They said that if I would come for another visit, they would cut a window in the wall for my comfort. Sure enough, when I returned two years later, that and other major improvements, including a brick veneer, had been completed.

Though the house had electricity, there was no indoor plumbing. The small bathroom and toilet enclosures were located outside, where a hand pump provided water. Several members of her family lived nearby, and her usually smiling daughter-in-law helped to prepare our meals.

Early the next morning while I was exercising outdoors, I noticed several young children watching me. It is possible that I was the first foreigner they had seen. Later that day I met the next door neighbor's son. He was about eight years old and spoke some English, the only one of the children who could. His young friends were eager to meet me, and together they acted as guides showing me around the village. When they learned of my religious interest, they took me to meet all of the neighbors who had built small shrines outdoors for a special observance dedicated to the Goddess Lakshmi. I was impressed with the artistic merit of some of the shrines, which appeared to be constructed of papier-mâché over a wooden frame.

At every home we visited, the owners invited me in for something to eat and drink. None of the villagers possessed much by Western standards, but they graciously shared whatever they had. I am not sure who had the best time, the children or I. Everywhere we went, two of them would hold onto each of my hands and others who were walking behind were eager to take their place. Some of the older children carried their smaller brothers and sisters.

To their delight, the Lakshmi festival entitles them to go around to all of the homes, where they are given special treats to eat. Carrying a bag much like American children on Halloween, they happily accept what they are given. I noticed that my host's mother included with her offering, the special sweets which I had brought to her.

Woman cutting vegetables on adz. It is held stationary by her foot. Saula, West Bengal.

Ferryboats. Village of Saula, West Bengal.

I called my head guide "Young Gopal," a name which Hindus use affectionately to refer to the deity Krishna, when he was a young boy. When Young Gopal saw me using my Swiss army knife one morning, he was impressed with its many blades and gadgets and asked me to give it to him. When my host's mother learned what he had done, she told him that he should never ask for anything of this world. Upon completion of my visit to the village, I did leave the knife with my host to give to Young Gopal's father, as a gift for his son when he was old enough to use it safely.

While combing my hair one day, Shymal's mother asked me to comb the hair (symbolically) of the statue of Krishna located on her altar. I knew in her own way, she was reminding me to keep God always in my mind and to dedicate all of my actions to the Divine. One morning I heard her chanting, and her son proudly informed me that his mother had memorized the 108 names for Krishna, and that was what she was singing. The number 108 has mystical significance to various religions. In a similar manner to Hinduism, Orthodox Judaism assigns God 108 attributes.

When Shymal and I were walking outside one evening, I heard voices and musical instruments coming from the other side of the village. I asked Shymal if we could go there, and he replied, "Of course." With the aid of a small flashlight, we headed in the direction of the music. About 15 villagers were crowded into a small house. A man beat the rhythm on an Indian drum with the palms of his hands. The lead female singer had a small pair of cymbals and a few other women had simple percussion "instruments." Though none of the villagers spoke English, it was not important, as they spoke the international language of devotion. I was grateful that I knew a chant in Bengali, because they asked me to sing for them. After the group finished chanting, a special meal was served to honor their spiritual teacher, and they asked us to join them.

The goal of traditional Hindu music is to stir the soul to attain union with God. Popular Western songs are usually inspired by sentiment or worldly experience and are composed to arouse the emotions. The Sanskrit word for "musician" is *bhagavathar*, "he who sings the praise of God." Classical Hindu music was composed to direct the consciousness inward. That is why chanting is often included as a part of meditation. Sharing in a Bengali *kirtan* (musical gathering) was another of the unique experiences of my Indian travels, and I will always remember the devotion of the villagers.

Man selling papaya, using rocks for weights. Market, village of Salua, West Bengal.

Two of group attending a Bengali kirtan (musical gathering). Saula, West Bengal.

West Bengal

Jute workers unconcerned by ominous monsoon sky. Mayapur, West Bengal.

After returning to Calcutta, I moved to a hotel within the city for my remaining few days. Calcutta's number of inhabitants per square mile is over 120,300 as compared to only 11,500 in New York City. Visiting in that overcrowded urban area was quite a contrast to the peaceful life of rural West Bengal.

The noisy sprawling metropolis has considerable urban problems, but what I remember most is its tranquil nature. Underneath the clamor of the city's commotion is a calmness. Even on crowded buses, if one focuses inwardly, peace emanates from everywhere.

Calcutta is a recent city by Indian standards, dating back about 300 years. The city is named after Kali Temple[1] (Kalikata), which was Anglicized to Calcutta. It was largely created by the British and was the capital of British India. Bengal became embroiled in the struggle for Indian Independence in the second half of the 19th century, which was an important factor in the capital's transfer to New Delhi in 1911. Because Bengal and the Punjab were the two primary regions of India with large mixed Hindu and Muslim populations, the land was divided between India and Pakistan. Partition probably affected Calcutta more than any other major Indian city.

The Victoria Memorial. Calcutta. Constructed 1906 - 1921.

The conflict between India and Pakistan in 1971 and the creation of Bangladesh led to another flood of refugees, worsening Calcutta's already overcrowded conditions. It is estimated that the city is home to six million refugees from famine and war.

I was told that Bengalis do not tolerate misbehavior towards women, and that it is generally safe for females to walk alone at night. Aside from their love for freedom, Bengalis are known for being extremely intelligent. Many of them are among India's leading poets and artists. Their movie industry is the largest in the world. It is quite sophisticated and is said to produce art films comparable to those made in the West.

While in Calcutta, I met the ex-Mr. India. The 58 year old man was still in good physical shape and traveled all over India to judge national contests. He introduced himself as the ex-Mr. India and said, "I am a muscleman. I know how to build muscles. But now I want to learn how to build the mind." After devoting his entire life to physical culture, he had learned that developing the body without the mind was of little value.

One of Calcutta's most noteworthy monuments from the British Raj period, the Victoria Memorial, is located downtown. The white marble museum has a huge dome and is situated at the southern end of a large green expanse known as the Maidan, which is almost two miles long and over a half mile wide.

I was eager to see if Mother Teresa was in the city. I went to the headquarters of her religious order, the Missionaries of Charity. An Indian nun told me that she was leaving on an international speaking tour early the next morning, but probably would attend chapel services that evening.

When I arrived at 6:30 p.m. for evening prayers, the dimly lighted chapel already was filled with nuns. They were kneeling on the concrete floor, spines erect and hands folded in supplication. They wore simple white cotton saris with their order's blue trim along the edges. Their head coverings were made of the same material. Most of them were Indians. Mother Teresa was not among them.

About 45 minutes later, I felt a magnetic force go through my body. I wondered if Mother Teresa had arrived. Turning my head to the rear, I saw the frail, petite woman enter. Though diminutive in stature, she is a spiritual giant. Without saying a word, her vibrations uplift the destitute and give hope to the despondent. Those with receptive hearts who come within her presence have their lives changed. She is indeed a living saint.

Prayer flags, Bhutia Busty Monastery, Buddhist. Darjeeling, 19th century. In background is Mt. Kanchenjunga, world's third tallest mountain.

Darjeeling: Queen of the Hills

Darjeeling is a fascinating "hill station," a term used by the British for their highland retreats which enabled them to escape from the scorching summer heat of the Indian plains. During my visit in March when the nights were still quite cold, I slept under four thick blankets. It is a peaceful town with beautiful cloud-capped mountain scenery. Straddling a ridge at an altitude of 6,400 feet, this town of under 100,000 people is surrounded on all sides by tea plantations built on steeply terraced mountainsides. Most of the buildings are wooden, some are dilapidated, and in the town itself, structures are crowded together. The upper parts of the town are joined to the lower areas by interconnecting narrow streets and flights of steps.

During my springtime visit, the Himalayan mountains were continually covered by mist and fog, except for a few hours at sunrise and just before sunset when nature abruptly lifted her veil as if by magic. During those times, the view of Mt. Kanchenjunga, the world's third highest mountain whose summit reaches 28,200 feet, was majestic.

Darjeeling was formerly called Dorje Ling, "Place of Thunderbolts." The British recognized its potential as a site for a "hill station," as well as its strategic importance of controlling a key pass leading into Nepal and Tibet. By the mid-19th century, the British annexed the region from the politically weakened Raja of Sikkim and soon established tea plantations which today produce some of the world's "highest" quality tea.

Today, Darjeeling has a diverse population of mountain people from all over the eastern Himalayas, which include many Tibetan refugees fleeing from China. It was refreshing to be in a different Indian culture where I could walk along the streets and have women of all ages greet me with a smile or salutation. In more traditional areas of India, Hindu women do not even make eye contact with men. I also enjoyed the food at Tibetan restaurants, which was not as highly seasoned as it is in most of India.

One of Darjeeling's most picturesque Buddhist monasteries, Bhutia Busty, is located a short walk down the mountainside from the main square. I had to ask directions several times, as the main walkways branched off in various directions. I arrived at the monastery late one evening. Large prayer flags fluttered noisily in the mountain winds. The 120 year old monastery's gold facade and deep red roof stood out in contrast to the stark white background of snow-covered Mt. Kanchenjunga.

Avalokitesvara, Lord of Compassion, with 1,000 arms. Gilt wood. Bhutia Busty Monastery, Darjeeling.

Terraced tea plantation, Himalayan Mountains. Darjeeling.

Ghoom Buddhist Monastery. Darjeeling.

Buddhist monk blowing ceremonial trumpet. The sound represents the Holy Spirit's presence in the universe. Ghoom Monastery. Darjeeling.

After the Chinese invasion, many high-ranking lamas came there as they fled Tibet, but today the monastery is staffed by younger monks, most of whom were in their late teens and early 20s. Because of my interest and understanding of Buddhism, I was invited for lunch the following day and to attend the afternoon meditation.

A young boy six or seven years old beat the different rhythms of the chants on a drum. During some of the more difficult rhythms, the monk leading the prayers placed his hand around the little boy's, to help him play the proper sequence of beats. For the most difficult portions, the monk played the drum himself. Once when the young boy rang the prayer bell at the wrong time, or more likely was playing with it out of restlessness, the monk gently took the bell from the child and placed it out of his reach. At the appropriate time, he gave the bell back to the little boy to ring. I was impressed by how well the young child beat the rhythms and how still he sat during the prayer period which lasted over one and a half hours.

After the prayer session was over, the monk, who was in his late 20s, asked me if I felt "special energy" from the chants. His question indicated to me that he had. From the amount of love and affection the monk gave to the child, I suspect that the young boy will elect to remain in the monastery when the time comes in his later teens to make that decision. While I was traveling in the neighboring state of Sikkim, I did meet a young man who had attended a Buddhist residential monastery school from ages 12 to 17. Though he enjoyed the monastic life and had his mother's approval, he was told that he had not progressed enough to join the order.

As I lay in bed that cold March night in Darjeeling, I gazed out my window towards the stars above the mountaintop and thought of the young boy who beat the ritual drum and rang the prayer bell. I reflected on the long road that lay before him, the path of inner discipline that he must master, and the normal childhood experiences he must forsake. I wondered if he would be able to withstand worldly temptation, or would even be asked to take monastic vows. I silently wished him well and then fell asleep.

The following morning, I had a cup of hot Darjeeling tea with breakfast. To my surprise, it tasted exactly like it does at home when I make it with a Twinings tea bag. Later, I walked into the town center and browsed in an antique shop in search of old Tibetan statuary. Three young girls of Chinese extraction entered. They were dressed in school uniforms, and probably attended the nearby Catholic school. They asked for money, and the shopkeeper, misunderstanding their purpose, told them to get out and quit begging. One replied to him in perfect English, but rudely, that the money was not for her, and she was not a beggar. It was for the poor people. I gave her a contribution and signed her donation book. Such outspoken language, I am sure, would not have occurred in Hindu India, where respect for one's elders is taught from birth.

At noon, I went to a small restaurant for lunch with a British traveler whom I had met. There were no empty tables so we asked two girls if we could join them, and they agreed. One of them was from Bangladesh and studying at a local college. After talking to her, I believed her to be of extremely high character, and gave her a substantial sum of money to contribute to her country's victims of a recent devastating flood. She assured me I would be sent a receipt, but I replied that it was unnecessary because had I not trusted her, I would not have made the contribution.

Upon my return to the United States, I had a letter from her father, a retired major general from the army. He told me he was pleased that I had trusted his daughter, and that he personally had handed the money to the President of Bangladesh. He also shared with the first lady how his daughter had received the money and they were all moved by the circumstances of the donation. He invited me to visit his country.

On a subsequent trip to India, I visited Darjeeling in early November. The weather was still warm and Mt. Kanchenjunga appeared to be only an arm's length away. The holiday of Diwali was about to commence. It is a festive celebration which dates back historically to the time when lamps were lighted to show Rama the way home after his period of exile. It symbolizes the triumph of good over evil.

In Darjeeling, it is the custom for a brother to honor his sister during Diwali, although in most of India, this tradition is observed on a different occasion. The practice has its roots in Hindu mythology when an evil supernatural being was trying to kill a woman's brother. She covered him with flowers to hide him, and this action saved his life. During Diwali the sister fasts all day until her brother arrives. She then places a garland of flowers around his neck and pours a ring of oil around him on the floor. As the oil is lighted, he stands encircled in flames, which symbolizes his sister's "ever-burning" protection. It is a very sentimental holiday. If one has no brother or sister, then that person tries to help and befriend someone as though he or she were a blood relative. I noticed several men proudly wearing their garlands in public.

*Men wearing garlands,
Festival of Diwali. Darjeeling.*

Hindu woman and child in front of Buddhist prayer flags. Note marking of "spiritual eye" on forehead.
Diwali Festival, Observatory Hill, Darjeeling.

A few days later, on the morning of Diwali, I went to Observatory Hill. It is situated adjacent to Darjeeling's town square at the top of a ridge. The park must have been named by the British, for its name belies its sacred use. The hill is holy to Hindus and Buddhists and has numerous shrines. Two of them are shared by members of both religions. A Buddhist priest sat on one side of the shrine and a Hindu pundit on the other. Hindu pilgrims went to the pundit to be blessed and to make their devotional offerings, while Buddhists approached their priest. I observed some worshipers who went to both the Hindu and Buddhist priests for their blessings.

Sikkim

Until a decade ago, it was difficult to secure a permit to visit Sikkim. I traveled around the country by bus, which enabled me to see the mountain scenery — and my first yaks which the farmers raise as livestock. As the bus slowly ascended the high mountain passes, it was as if I were viewing the terraced landscapes and green valleys below from an airplane. From mountain altitudes of 28,000 feet where peaks are capped in snow all year, the terrain tapers down to a dense rain forest that lies at sea level.

Little is known of Sikkim's history before the 17th century. In 1640, it became an independent monarchy. Sikkim controlled a key pass between India and Tibet, which is one of the reasons why the British made it a protectorate in 1861. Nepalis began migrating into Sikkim after 1870. Most of the Nepalis who came to Sikkim were Hindu, and today they comprise the largest ethnic group, making up about 70 percent of the population. The people of Sikkim voted to become a state of India in May, 1975.

Pelling/Pemayangtse Monastery

By far the most beautiful views of the Himalayan Mountains that I had seen in all of India were from the small town of Pelling, also in the state of Sikkim. Mt. Kanchenjunga and the other peaks at sunrise and sunset provided a magnificent panorama. Billowing clouds often obscured the view during the day, but as the sun set in the late afternoon, a soft red glow illuminated them.

Located about a mile from Pelling is one of Sikkim's oldest and most important monasteries. It was founded in 1705 and belongs to the Tantric Nyingmapa sect, established in the 8th century by the famous Indian teacher Padmasambhava. The monastery looks out on the snow-capped Himalayan range containing Mt. Kanchenjunga. Inside are impressive Tantric wall paintings and large Buddhist statuary. The building was severely damaged during two 20th century earthquakes and since has been restored.

The Pelling area offers scenic places to hike. There is a nearby lake which is an ideal spot for a picnic. I particularly enjoyed a short walk to a small, peaceful mountaintop monastery where the two resident monks lived a life of seclusion. When the monastery is shrouded in mist and clouds, it appears as if it is floating in heaven.

Darjeeling dwarfed by towering Himalayan Mountains of West Sikkim.

Young monks in training. Rumtek Monastery, near Gangtok. Sikkim.

Gangtok/Rumtek Monastery

I did not remain overnight in Gangtok, the small capital of Sikkim. It is the only large city in that remote mountainous state of under a half million people. I opted instead for the tranquility of the nearby Rumtek Monastery, located 15 miles away. It was dusk when my taxi arrived, and nature had cloaked the gounds in her mystic mantle of peace. After arranging to stay at a small hotel which was managed by a Tibetan Buddhist family, I went immediately to the prayer hall. It was a recent structure, with colorful murals that covered most of the walls. The following morning, the family who ran the hotel invited me to have a simple breakfast with them. Afterwards, I spent a pleasant day visiting other small monasteries and hiking on the mountainside.

Orissa

The three temple towns of Puri, Bhubaneswar and Konarak with its great Sun Temple are situated close to each other in the state of Orissa. Bhubaneswar is on the heavily traveled Calcutta-Madras railway line. When I went to buy a ticket in Calcutta for this journey they were sold out, and I had to go to a special office for foreigners. Fortunately, there is a national railway policy of holding back a percentage of tickets for non-Indians. Otherwise, traveling by train often would have been impossible since the multitudes of Indians often reserve their tickets far in advance.

Bhubaneswar

Bhubaneswar has some excellent Orissan style temples. Their ornately carved bee-hive towers curve gently inward as they reach the top. Local guides proudly claim that at one time the city had over 7,000 temples, of which hundreds still stand. Most of them date from the 8th to 13th century, with the largest and most famous being Lingaraj, which dates from circa 1000 A.D.

Woman in early morning devotion outside Orissan temple. Bhubaneswar.

Konarak

About 40 miles from Bhubaneswar is the Sun Temple at Konarak, dedicated to the Sun God Surya. This masterpiece of Medieval Orissan architecture has been designated a United Nations (UNESCO) World Heritage site. Constructed from 1238 to 1264, it was probably never completed. It is famous for the huge intricate chariot wheels which are carved around the base of the temple. Their spokes serve as sundials, whose shadows give the precise time. The temple was conceived as a gigantic representation of the sun god's chariot and is pulled by seven sculptured horses. Its sandstone pyramidal roof soars over 100 feet and is a landmark for sailors far out in the Bay of Bengal. Like the temples at Khajuraho, Surya Temple at Konarak is covered with erotic sculptures. Konarak also may have been a center for a Tantric cult.

Huge chariot wheels carved around base of Surya Temple at Konarak. Eastern Ganga Dynasty, ca. 1240.

Statue of the Sun God Surya at Surya Temple. Konarak. Eastern Ganga Dynasty, ca. 1240.

Children doing school work in outdoor class. Konarak.

◁ *Opposite
Sadhu (ascetic),
Bhubaneswar.*

Puri

Twenty miles down the coast from Konarak is Puri, home of Jagannath Temple. This seaside town is the site of one of India's greatest annual events held each summer. The *Rath Yatra* consists of huge "temple cars," or massive floats, which require over 4,000 men to pull them down a broad avenue to a destination over a half mile away.

I arrived in Puri on the second day of the Spring festival of Holi. Unknown to me, hardly anyone escapes being sprinkled with colored waters and powders, so it is wise not to wear good clothing during that period. Some say the holiday's tradition of playfully throwing colored water on others stems from similar pranks that young Krishna played on the *gopis* (milkmaids) over 3,500 years ago.

I hired a bicycle rickshaw to take me to Jagannath Temple. I had on my best white Indian attire. One can imagine the inviting target I was to the children, a foreigner dressed in white and sitting on the seat of a passing open rickshaw! When the children came to spray me with colored water, I raised my hand and asked them please not to. One small boy said in pidgin English "little-little" so I told him okay. When I realized that the red dye had ruined my shirt, I smiled and told them to go ahead — which they gleefully did. From then on, I was fair game for all, and I happily became a target for their squirt guns. Some of the local ruffians must have used paint because it took almost a week to get the dyes out of my hair. I still have those color-stained clothes which look like a tie-dyed, designer-styled outfit.

While I was standing in front of Jagannath Temple, two village women approached me, one of whom was carrying a baby. She took the baby's finger and touched me at the point between my eyebrows, the spiritual eye. Perhaps they had never seen a light-skinned Westerner before and they were just blessing a guest in their country on a holiday. Not knowing the purpose of her blessing, I accepted it as being from God.

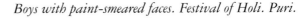

Boys with paint-smeared faces. Festival of Holi. Puri.

Street vendor splattered with paint, Festival of Holi. Puri.

Hindu ladies wading in surf. Puri.

I stayed at a hotel on Puri's white sandy beaches, but the sun was so bright that I had to avoid sunbathing during the hottest times of the day. While walking on the beach near a tiny fishing village, I noticed that some boats had been pulled onto dry land. They were built in several sections which were bound together. They had been hewn from heavy tree trunks and split lengthwise. It was the wood's bulk which provided the boat's buoyancy. When they were not in use, they were taken apart to dry.

While I was in the ocean, I noticed that most of the younger women who waded into the surf were fully clothed, although I did see a few middle-aged women in conservative one piece bathing suits. The females whom I recall most vividly were a group of four attractive college-age girls in their fine saris. It was refreshing to be in a culture where women do not blatantly use sex appeal to attract men and virginity is still valued at marriage.

When I returned to India in 1993, I was surprised to see in big cities that sensual female forms had become part of the advertising on sign boards, where sex appeal is now routinely being used to sell a manufacturer's products. I wondered if the sexual revolution and its overall negative effects on social values could be far behind. How quickly thousands of years of tradition are discarded.

Buddha's Enlightenment at Bodh Gaya

Bodh Gaya is easy to reach because the railroad junction at nearby Gaya is on the main Delhi-Calcutta line. Even with a reservation, it is a hassle trying to board a train in overcrowded conditions. I would have traveled by rail less than I did, were it not for the abundance of porters who were always available to take my luggage aboard. On this day I did not have a seat reservation. My first class, "non-reserved" ticket to Gaya entitled me to sit wherever I could — if I could. Since it was a day journey, I was not concerned. "Getting there" in India may not be half the fun, but it is half of the experience.

When my train arrived, it had only one first class car, and all of the seats were already occupied. The first compartment I peered into had so many peanut shells on the floor that I thought surely I must be in second class. A sympathetic group in another compartment saw me searching for a seat and motioned to me to come in. To make room for me and a rather stout English woman who was also seeking a seat, an older Indian woman sat on the floor on a large rolled carpet she had purchased, and a younger lady squeezed in on the other side. A woman, two men, two teen-age girls and a child were now sitting in a space designed to comfortably seat three. We had all paid the same ticket fares, yet they packed together like sardines. Their thoughtfulness reinforced my respect for Hindu culture, and I hoped under similar circumstances Americans would be as courteous to foreigners.

The family sitting across from me was from South India. They had made a pilgrimage to Banaras. Each of them was so peaceful and radiant that they made a deep impression on me. The two teen-age girls would smile whenever I looked at them, and we played a game of hiding our faces from each other in mock embarrassment. The oldest, who was absolutely beautiful, made more eye contact with me than any other girl had done in all of India. Perhaps it was okay because of the circumstances. A man in the compartment shared cookies that his wife had made, and also bought the English woman and me tea when a vendor came aboard at one of the stations. Another man was eager to talk, and I was glad the English woman was there to entertain him because I wished for some quiet time.

The train arrived in Gaya shortly after 10 p.m. I walked across the street to the nearest and nicest hotel in the town, which by Western standards was basic at best. I ordered a bucket of hot water which arrived tepid. I then took an Indian-style bath by squatting and pouring water over my body with the small plastic cup which is provided along with a bucket in all bathrooms. By now I had become adept at pouring the water over my head and shoulders in such a skillful manner that the water would trickle down my entire body, wasting hardly a precious drop. After bathing, I went to bed.

The next morning, I was eager to make the eight mile trip to Bodh Gaya where the Buddha had become enlightened 25 centuries ago. For that reason, Bodh Gaya is supreme among all the holy places of the Buddhists, and is to them what Banaras is to the Hindus — the most sacred place of pilgrimage.

The large sacred Bodhi (banyan) tree shading the spot where Siddhartha (Buddha's former name) gained enlightenment through meditation is not the original tree under which he sat. A sapling from the original tree was taken to Sri Lanka (Ceylon) by Emperor Ashoka's daughter when he brought Buddhism there. That tree still flourishes at Anuradhapura in Sri Lanka, and one of its saplings was brought back to Bodh Gaya where it now grows.

Near the sacred spot is Mahabodhi Temple, which was built in the 11th century. Its pyramidal spire rises over 150 feet, and is similar to an earlier structure which was built on the same site. As I passed under the east gateway and through a long courtyard, the superstructure dominated the view. Equally impressive were the strong vibrations of peace which I could feel immediately.

The name Buddha means "The Enlightened One." He was born about 556 B.C. in northern India on the southern border of present-day Nepal.[2] His father was a rajah of the warrior caste (*Kshatriyas*). The young Hindu prince's full name was Siddhartha Gautama of the Shakyas. Siddhartha (meaning "he who has achieved his goal") was his given name. Gautama (traditionally a *Brahmin* family name) was his surname, and Shakya was the name of his family's clan. When he became the Buddha at age 35, he was called Shakyamuni, sage of the Shakyas, symbolizing something beyond which could be said and thought.

Mahabodhi Temple, Bodh Gaya.
11th century.

Bodh Gaya, Bihar

Monk chanting in front of carved stone railing, Mahabodhi Temple. Bodh Gaya.

Tibetan pilgrims praying under Bodhi Tree, site of Buddha's enlightenment. Bodh Gaya.

At Siddhartha's birth, the astrologers gave his father a disturbing prophecy about his son: he would become either a great emperor or on beholding the "Four Signs" (an old man; a sick man; a corpse; and a mendicant holy man, a *sadhu*), he would become an equally famous ascetic. His father was determined that Siddhartha must never see anything which might cause him to be dissatisfied with courtly life and restricted him to the palace compound. He made continuous efforts to keep the young prince's mind attached to the world and surrounded him with every conceivable luxury. At age 16, Siddhartha was married to a beautiful and devoted princess, who bore him a son.

Siddhartha grew into manhood thinking of the world as a place for endless happy events. But the prince also was curious about the world outside the palace grounds. One day with his charioteer Channa, Siddhartha disobeyed his father's strict commands never to leave the palace compound and secretly went to the nearby villages to see the world. On three successive outings, the handsome prince was shocked to the very depths of his being to see for the first time in his life a shriveled-looking old man, a dying man and a corpse. He discovered that life was not as he had been taught to believe when he had been surrounded by his protective family within the walled confines of his luxurious palace.

On the fourth journey after seeing a monk with shaven head and ochre robe, Siddhartha's inner conflict became so great that he decided to renounce forever his sheltered and luxurious life. One night while everyone in the palace was asleep, he departed with a heavy heart on his "Great Going Forth" in search of truth which would give him complete understanding and mastery over the mystery of life and death.

For seven years the prince practiced many austerities. Once he grew so weak from lack of food that he fainted. This experience taught him that asceticism alone was not the way to enlightenment, but it was through the human body that man was to attain illumination. With this realization, Siddhartha gave up mortification and replaced it with the "Middle Way." The body is given precisely the food and rest it needs for optimum functioning, but nothing more. He is credited with saying: "...for the physical body of man lives only from day to day; if you supply it with what it actually needs, you will still have time to meditate, while if you seek to supply it with all it wants the task is without end." The Buddha taught that by the "Middle Way" the wise person avoided both extremes of asceticism and self-indulgence as one follows a balanced life of calm detachment. He then began the final phase of his quest for enlightenment through concentrated thought and scientific meditation similar to the path of *Raja Yoga*.

One evening while meditating under a banyan tree which is now known as the "Bodhi Tree," or "Tree of Wisdom," Siddhartha sensed that he was on the verge of enlightenment and vowed not to move until he obtained illumination. After remaining in meditation for 49 days and enduring many tests and hardships, salvation came. Declaring, "I will beat the drum of the Immortal in the darkness of the world," he arose from his seat under the "Bodhi Tree" and went to the Deer Park near Sarnath where he preached his first sermon to his former companions in austerities.

For the next 50 years the Buddha traveled over much of the basin of the Ganges. He shared with thousands his "Middle Path" to liberation or *nirvana*.

His teachings include the "Four Noble Truths," the "Noble Eightfold Path," and the "Wheel of the Law." According to the Buddha, the principal cause of suffering is desire. He taught and accepted peasants and noblemen alike, regardless of their caste, and organized the original Buddhist orders of monks and nuns.

"The Four Noble Truths" are: 1. life is suffering; 2. the reason for suffering is desire; 3. suffering must be caused to cease by overcoming desire; 4. suffering will cease if one finds the path to deliverance, which is the "Eightfold Path." The elements of the "Eightfold Path" are: 1. right knowledge or understanding; 2. right purpose or resolve; 3. right speech; 4. right conduct or action; 5. right occupation or a livelihood conducive to salvation, preferably the monastic life; 6. right effort; 7. right awareness or self-mastery; and 8. right meditation.

The Buddha used the "Wheel of the Law" allegory to illustrate the certainty of *karma*. Its symbol, the wheel, was a visual reminder of his teaching:

> That which ye sow, ye reap. See yonder fields!
> The sesamum was sesamum, the corn
> was corn. The silence and the Darkness knew!
> So is man's fate born.
> He cometh, reaper of the things he sowed....

Buddhism is an offshoot of Hinduism, and rightly understood, the teachings are similar. Interestingly, Hinduism claims the Buddha to be the ninth incarnation of Vishnu, but perhaps it is just as well that Buddhism became a separate religion. By putting the purest Hindu wisdom into a simpler form, Buddhism has spread beyond India throughout Southeast Asia, and has reached populations less keenly metaphysical, who might not have been receptive to the ancient Hindu faith.

Buddhist monks prostrating in prayer.
Bodh Gaya.

Gilded Buddhas in base of Mahabodhi Temple at spot
where Siddhartha became enlightened. Bodh Gaya.

Praying monk, Buddhist monastery. Bodh Gaya.

Gaya

Just as Bodh Gaya is a principal pilgrimage site for Buddhists, nearby Gaya is a center for Hindu pilgrims. Twelve miles north of Gaya are the ancient Barabar caves, which are the "Marabar" caves of E. M. Forster's <u>A Passage to India</u>.

When I visited the sacred Vishnupad Temple in Gaya, I was looking forward to seeing the footprint of Vishnu which is said to be inside. At a few Hindu temples, because of the disrespect shown during periods of foreign occupation, non-Hindus are not allowed to enter. When I was refused admittance, I replied that I was a vegetarian and practitioner of Hindu yoga. A man standing nearby insisted that I be allowed inside.

He escorted me to the various altars and showed me the proper way to offer the flowers which I had purchased from a small boy. At the most sacred shrines inside, there were the usual devotional pushing and shoving pilgrims who numbered at least twice too many for the space. To get to the statue of Vishnu was almost impossible. I offered my devotion at his "footprint" which is imprinted in a solid rock and surrounded by a silver-plated basin. The "footprint" was covered with a clouded liquid, which appeared to be a mixture of water, milk and oil, and had many flowers floating on its surface. I was told the 16 inch "footprint" could only be viewed at night. Since I was expecting to see Vishnu's real footprint, I stood there feeling embarrassed for being so gullible. I had a similar experience at a temple in Thailand, where I had keenly anticipated seeing a real footprint of the Buddha.

Rajgir and Nalanda

I was so inspired by the sanctity of Bodh Gaya that I decided to visit two Buddhist pilgrimage sites about 50 miles away. Late one afternoon I took a bus to Rajgir, where the Buddha spent 12 years of his life. It was about 10:00 p.m. when the bus arrived, and the little town of a few thousand people was shrouded in darkness. Someone gave me directions to the Tourist Bungalow where I spent the night and arranged for a guide for the following morning.

I was awakened early the next morning by the guide's knock on my door. He informed me that he had a full day of sightseeing planned for me so I got dressed quickly and skipped breakfast. My guide and I boarded a bus for the 12 mile trip to Nalanda, which once was a great center of Buddhist culture. It reached its peak of fame in the 5th century A.D. Leading scholars from China, Korea, Japan, Mongolia, Tibet and Ceylon came there to study. The university once housed 10,000 students and was considered to offer the highest postgraduate education in all Asia. The expenses for this monastic school were met by royal grants and endowments from the wealthy. The center flourished for 700 years until the monastery, university and library were sacked and burned by Muslims in 1205.

I had no idea the excavated ruins would be so extensive. The Great Stupa reminded me of an Egyptian pyramid. Its many steps allowed us to walk to the top and offered an excellent view of the surrounding countryside. My guide told me that the Buddha had worshiped here and had placed floral offerings near the top in memory of a disciple who was his good friend.

I noticed a number of village women walking towards the nearby community. When I asked my guide where they were going, he replied that it was a special day. They were heading to the Sun Temple to make petitions to God. Many carried a brass or copper container filled with what appeared to be milk to be used as an offering. When I asked if we could visit the temple, he said of course.

As we approached the temple, there was a steady line of petite, wet, shivering women streaming into the courtyard. They had bathed at a site perhaps a quarter of a mile away. On a freezing day in which I had on my warmest clothing, they had on nothing more than thin wet cotton saris and shawls.

Inside, many of the women were making the traditional ritual circle around the interior of the temple. Then they poured the milky liquid from their vessels on a large, black stone sculpture of Vishnu. They stood silently offering their prayers to God. I was impressed by their devotion.

When we returned to Rajgir, my guide engaged a two wheel horse-drawn cart to take us to a mountain made sacred by the presence of the Buddha. On the uphill grade, the driver used a whip to beat his horse on the under-belly. I could not stand the cruelty so I asked my guide to tell him to stop and remind him that the Buddha had taught compassion for all beings, including animals. Still he continued whipping the horse who pulled as hard as he could.

I remembered a story of when the Buddha was passing through a village and saw a goat which was about to be sacrificed. He placed his own head on the chopping block and asked that he be killed instead. Touched by his compassion, many in the village became his disciples. With my guide as interpreter, I asked the driver to whip me instead of the horse. When he later hit the horse again, I had my guide ask him if he were a horse, would he want "himself" as his owner. He stopped after that.

About half way up the mountain, our cart had to pull off the narrow road to make way for a vehicle. As we stopped and waited, I became so engulfed in a wave of peace that I thought: "What is this?" As we pulled back onto the road to continue our journey, I noticed a small sign that said the Buddha often rested here on his way to the mountain top. I was grateful for the circumstance which necessitated that we stop there.

We also visited the Bamboo Garden where the Buddha lived for three years. Nearby is a Japanese monastery where a young monk beat a large drum every few seconds to awaken souls from the sleep of delusion. The rhythmic drumbeat shattered the silence and produced a haunting sound.

We walked to a hot sulphur springs crowded with people who took advantage of the unlimited source of heated water. It could be the only hot bath they would ever have. Behind it were steps leading up to a cave where it is believed that after the Buddha's death, the First Buddhist Council met to write down his teachings. Before hiking up the mountain to the cave, I, too, enjoyed a bath in the hot mineral springs.

I visited one other Buddhist pilgrimage site of importance located in the adjacent state of Uttar Pradesh near Gorakhpur. Kushinagar is thought to be the place where the Buddha died and entered into *nirvana*.

Regardless of one's religion, the principal sites connected with the life of the Buddha are worth visiting. They have a special peacefulness and sanctity about them.

Pilgrim, Gorakhnath Temple. Gorakhpur, Uttar Pradesh.

Opposite▷
Men and boys enjoying hot springs. Rajgir, Bihar.

Reclining Buddha, signifying his entrance into nirvana. Kushinagar, Uttar Pradesh. Gilded wood, silk.

Taj Mahal. Tomb erected by Shah Jahan for his wife, Mumtaz Mahal. Agra, 1631-1653.

Chapter Three

The North

Delhi Union Territory, Uttar Pradesh, Himachal Pradesh, Jammu and Kashmir, Punjab, and Haryana

India's rich cultural diversity is most evident in the North. The Punjab is predominantly Sikh. Jammu and Kashmir has a large Muslim population and the remaining states are overwhelmingly Hindu. A multicultural society presents India — and indeed the world — with the challenge of proving that large populations of different faiths can live harmoniously under one government. India is the great social experiment of the twentieth century. Its outcome will influence the fate of the world.

Uttar Pradesh is India's most populous state. It is one of the states stretching across northern India in what is called the "Hindi belt," where Hindi is the predominant language. Though most of Uttar Pradesh is a vast plain, the northwestern region includes the Himalayan mountains and the glacial source of the Ganges River. Located in the foothills are the important pilgrimage towns of Rishikesh and Hardwar which are built upon the banks of India's most sacred river. As the Ganges flows across the plains it passes Allahabad, one of the four cities which hosts a huge religious festival, the *Kumbha Mela*. Eighty-five miles east of Allahabad is Banaras (Varanasi), India's holiest city. Nearby is the Buddhist pilgrimage site of Sarnath. With such diversity, everyone will find something memorable in this state.

◁ *Opposite*
Early morning fog in Garhwal Himalayan Mountains
near Badrinath. Chandrapuri.

*Woman wearing traditional jewelry.
Kangra district, Himachal Pradesh.*

Much of the state of Himachal Pradesh is covered by the Himalayan mountains. Located in picturesque settings are several cities which are well-known in the West. Simla was the British "summer capital" and Dharamsala is the Dalai Lama's home in exile from China. Both are "hill stations" and are built on steep mountains. The beautiful Kulu Valley, with snow-capped Himalayan peaks forming its background, is called the "Valley of the Gods."

India's northernmost state has a double name, Jammu and Kashmir. Jammu is in the south. Its geography is a transition from the plains of India to the Himalayas. Further north is the Vale of Kashmir, a large Himalayan valley where the people are predominantly Muslim. Located in the remote northeastern part of the state is a high plateau known as Ladakh. Its culture is primarily Buddhist and Tibetan, which is in stark contrast to Kashmir and the rest of India.

The majority of India's Sikhs live in the Punjab. Located on India's northwestern border with Pakistan, it was partitioned at Independence. The population included large numbers of Muslims, Sikhs and Hindus. The region was divided into the Muslim state of Punjab which became part of Pakistan, and a Sikh and Hindu Punjab which remained part of India. Horrible atrocities took place in 1948 as millions of Sikhs and Hindus migrated eastward and millions of Muslims fled westward to the newly formed Pakistan. In 1966, the Indian Punjab was divided again, creating the largely Hindi speaking state of Haryana and the predominantly Sikh, Punjabi-speaking state of Punjab.

Old and New Delhi

Today's Old Delhi, as the name indicates, is built upon old cities and mixed traditions. Archaeologists have unearthed seven municipalities dating back 800 years, although legend links the founding of Delhi to the ancient heroes of the <u>Mahabharata</u>, 5,000 years ago.

Old Delhi served as the capital of Muslim India most of the time between the 12th and 19th centuries. Many of the city's mosques, forts and bazaars date to the mid-17th century. In contrast, present-day New Delhi is a city of broad boulevards, landscaped gardens and neoclassical buildings. The imperial city is a creation of the British, who began its construction in 1911 and inaugurated it as the capital of India in 1931. Today, the city is part of the Delhi Union Territory, a federal district similar to Washington D.C.

The British were not the first Europeans to establish trading posts in India. They were preceded by the Portuguese, French and Dutch. It was under the hegemony of the East India Company that the British established spheres of influence in Madras in the South, Bombay in the West and Calcutta in the East. By the beginning of the 19th century, the London based East India Company virtually ruled India.

The British captured Delhi in 1803. During the Indian Mutiny of 1857-1858, Delhi was a center of resistance to the British and the city was ransacked. The uprising, in which thousands were killed, ended the East India Company's dominance and led to its dissolution. Soon afterwards, India formally became a part of the British Empire and a Viceroy was appointed to represent the Queen. British rule was administered from Calcutta during that early period.

In 1877, Queen Victoria was proclaimed Empress of India in Delhi. George V came to India to be crowned emperor in 1911. It was he who suggested that the "Indian style" be incorporated into the new imperial city to be built at New Delhi so Indians could identify with it.

At the center of New Delhi is the Presidential Palace, the Rashtrapati Bhawan. The red sandstone mansion is built in the classical style, but its huge central rotunda resembles a Buddhist *stupa* more than a Roman dome. Its 340 rooms are arranged around a dozen courtyards and once required 2,000 people for its upkeep. When completed in 1929, the cost was more than 12 million pounds. It was in Durbar Hall where the imperial throne is located that Lord Mountbatten, the last British Viceroy, granted India its independence at the stroke of midnight of August 14-15, 1947. Jawaharlal Nehru became India's first prime minister.

Groom approaching wedding reception on horseback, a Hindu tradition. New Delhi.

Iron pillar, perhaps 2,000 years old, which has never rusted. Legend says that if you can encircle it with your arms while standing with your back to it, your wish will come true. Qutab Minar Complex, New Delhi suburb.

Groundskeeper posing with cow-powered lawn mower. Safdarjang Tomb, New Delhi. 1753 - 1754.

Until recently, the Nehru family had provided all of the major prime ministers of India: Nehru, his daughter Indira Gandhi (who was no relation to Mahatma Gandhi), and her son Rajiv. Both of the Gandhis were assassinated while in office in reprisal for the actions they took to solve difficult political situations.

The dichotomy of modern India is mirrored in the striking differences between Old Delhi and New Delhi. On my many visits to Delhi, I would rotate my hotel stays between New Delhi's fashionable Connaught Place and the city's old bazaars. The narrow steets of Old Delhi often were jammed with people browsing at small shops and street markets. Each section of the bazaar had its unique smell. Had I been blindfolded, I could have detected the newly dyed cotton textiles or over-ripe fruit. I loved the aroma of the spice markets, and best of all was passing by a shop where my favorite sandalwood incense was burning.

There was seldom enough room for pedestrians in the bazaars during peak periods. They were particularly crowded in the evening, and it was impossible not to be jostled. When an automobile or rickshaw passed, we all had to scamper out of their way, standing as close as possible to buildings, whose walls delineated the streets.

What I remember most about New Delhi is the typically British-looking architecture. Anyone who goes there will remember the graceful colonnades and huge circular design of Connaught Place, and the radial roads that originate from it.

To visit the famous Mughal monuments of the two disjointed cities, I took an all-day bus tour. In the morning we visited the tomb of the Mughal emperor Humayun, built by his wife in the mid-16th century. Most art historians agree that the large, squat building with high arched entrances, bulbous dome and formal gardens is the forerunner of the Taj Mahal. The tour also went to Safdarjang Tomb, constructed in 1753-1754. It is one of the last monumental examples of Mughal architecture before the empire collapsed. Jami Mosque, said to be the largest mosque in India and the second largest in the world, is the final architectural undertaking of Shah Jahan, the builder of the Taj Mahal. Its courtyard which is enclosed by high walls can accommodate 25,000 worshipers. Constructed from red sandstone and white marble, it is flanked on either side by two tall minarets. In the mosque's shrine for sacred relics, the keeper showed me a strand of hair said to be Mohammed's.

Jami Mosque, the largest in India. Old Delhi. 1644 - 1658.

Rickshaw driver enjoying company of school children. Agra.

The tour concluded with a visit to the Red Fort, whose red sandstone walls extend for over a mile. Its construction was begun by Shah Jahan, who inherited an overflowing treasury of gold, silver and precious jewels, which enabled him to create Mughal India's most lavish extravaganzas. The "Hall of Private Audiences" once was luxurious, having contained the magnificent Peacock Throne which was carted off to Iran in 1739 by a Persian conqueror. At the top of the solid gold throne were figures of peacocks whose translucent colors emanated from inlaid sapphires, rubies, emeralds and other precious stones. Though the silver ceiling had been stripped, the perfect symmetry of the chamber's onion-domed arches and columns preserved an aura of its bygone splendor. Inscribed above a marble screen is the famous Persian couplet:

If there is a paradise on earth
It is this, it is this, it is this.

Bicycle rickshaw driver taking children home after school. Book bags are on top. New Delhi.

Loaded camels passing behind Taj Mahal, as viewed from across Yamuna River near Red Fort. Agra.

Agra: The Taj Mahal — Jewel of the East

One of India's finest trains, the air-conditioned and super-fast Shatabdi Express links Delhi to Agra. The 125 mile journey takes only two hours, and it leaves Delhi early in the morning for the convenience of tourists making a day trip.

Agra was the capital of India during the Mughal Empire in the 16th and 17th centuries, and I was eager to visit the magnificent monuments which date from that era. The city of over a million is located on the west bank of the Yamuna River. In addition to the Taj Mahal and Agra Fort, there are several impressive Muslim tombs. In order to visit them, I hired a motor rickshaw for the remainder of the day. To reach the tomb of Akbar the Great, we had to cross over the Yamuna River on a narrow bridge. A steady flow of cars, rickshaws, bullock carts and pedestrians resulted in a continual traffic jam.

After a pleasant ride through the countryside, we arrived at the mausoleum of the Muslim Emperor Akbar the Great. The tomb's construction was begun by Akbar, but it was his son Jehangir who completed the memorial to his religiously tolerant father in 1613. The red sandstone structure is inlaid with white marble and has a three story minaret rising from each corner. The tomb has a combination of Islamic and Hindu architectural styles. Four red sandstone gates lead to the grounds. One gate has Muslim motifs, one has Hindu, one has Christian and one is Akbar's creative mixture.

Akbar was a complex individual. He came to the throne at the age of fourteen when his father died. Though he never learned to read or write, he is said to have remembered every word read to him. He took drawing lessons as a boy and developed a great appreciation for art. He enjoyed the outdoors and had a fondness for dangerous sports including elephant fighting, yet he loved art, music and poetry.

Akbar had a Hindu guru and was tolerant of other religions including Hindus, Jains, Christians and Parsis, followers of the teachings of Zarathustra from Persia. He rejected traditional Islam and founded a new religion (Din-i-Illali) which synthesized wisdom from all of the major religions. Without Akbar's tolerance to his non-Muslim subjects, the success of the Mughal empire would not have been possible. Though Hindus and Muslims were not interested in his idealistic attempts to promote religious unity, his deserted royal city Fatehpur Sikri remains a living memorial to his noble effort.

Agra, Uttar Pradesh

After leaving Akbar's tomb, I returned to Agra to visit the squat mausoleum of Itimad-ud-Daula. The short minarets at each of the tomb's four corners, foreshadowed elements which would reach perfection in the design of the Taj. The Persian buried here was the emperor's chief minister. His beautiful daughter married Emperor Jehangir, son of Akbar the Great, and she became known as Nur Jahan, the "light of the world."

I waited until late afternoon to visit the Taj Mahal. The world famous Mughal monument was erected by Emperor Shah Jahan in memory of his beautiful wife Mumtaz Mahal, who died in childbirth in 1629 after having given him fourteen children, only seven of whom survived.

Shah Jahan, whose title means King of the World, has the reputation of being the greatest builder of all the Indian emperors. Construction of the Taj employed 20,000 workers from India and Central Asia and took 22 years. It was completed in 1653. The scaffolding supposedly cost as much as the structure due to a lack of wood necessitating that it be made of stone. The main architect came from Shiraz in Iran, and artisans were imported from France and Italy to assist with the decoration.

It is said that Shah Jahan had intended to build a second Taj in black marble across the river for his own tomb, a negative image of the white Taj. But before he could embark on this project, he was deposed by his son Aurangzeb, just as he had done to his father, Jehangir. Shah Jahan spent the rest of his life as a prisoner in the Agra Fort, looking across the river at his lavish memorial to his favorite wife, who had died three years after he came to the throne.

The Taj Mahal is one of the most beautifully proportioned buildings in the world and retains its symmetry from any angle. It reduces Persian and Indian styles to an elegant and simple form. The building's details are also impressive with inlaid semi-precious stones forming designs in a process known as *pietra dura*. Like the Grand Canyon in Arizona, the Taj becomes different with the changing light, and even though I had seen many pictures of it, standing in its presence was exhilarating.

The next day I went to Agra Fort, which was begun by Akbar in 1565. The huge fort with its red sandstone walls looked similar to the Red Fort at Old Delhi. Initially a military edifice, it became more luxurious by the time of Shah Jahan, the builder of the Taj. The fort's marble "Pearl" Mosque was built by Shah Jahan between 1446 and 1463. It is considered to be perfectly proportioned, and a Persian inscription inside the mosque compares it to a flawless pearl.

Taj Mahal reflecting pink glow of sun's last rays. Agra. Constructed 1631 - 1653.

Mathura

Located close to Agra are the holy cities of Mathura and Brindaban. Both municipalities were made sacred by the presence of Krishna during his early life. Many Hindus consider Krishna to be India's greatest human expression of Divinity and they cherish the anecdotes of his mischievous childhood.

Mathura has a long history of multiculturalism. When I visited its museum, there was a wide variety of sculptures from the different religions and cultures which once dominated the area. Prior to the arrival of the Buddhists of the Kushan dynasty from Northern India almost 2,000 years ago, the city had been a religious center to the Jains. Buddhism continued to flourish in Mathura with the rise of the powerful new Gupta empire about 320 A.D. It was the Gupta civilization which produced the great Sanskrit writer Kalidasa, and it also was during this period that India's earliest surviving paintings were created on the walls of the Buddhist caves at Ajanta.

Legend has it that Krishna's parents were held captives in a prison, where the infant was born over 3,500 years ago. They had been imprisoned because of a prophecy that they would give birth to a son who would grow up to overthrow the evil king Kansa. All of their children were put to death at birth, but Krishna miraculously survived. The story closely parallels the prophecy of the birth of Jesus and the "Slaughter of the Innocent" in which Herod massacred guiltless children for similar reasons.

The site of the Kesava Deo Temple, built on the spot where Lord Krishna is said to have been born, is covered by a mosque erected in 1661. I was told by my guide that in keeping with the tradition of Muslim conquests at that time, the sacred Hindu temple was destroyed and a mosque was constructed in its place. Hindus are allowed to worship in a simple basement shrine, where no images of Krishna are allowed.

Brindaban

Brindaban with its famous temples dedicated to Lord Krishna is located about six miles north of Mathura. That is where the mischievous child Krishna played tricks on the *gopis* (milkmaids), and it is a favorite site for Hindus. When we arrived, there were several bus loads of pilgrims who had made the long, arduous trip from Nepal. They had come to honor Krishna, whose Bhagavad Gita is the most beloved scripture of India.

Krishna brought essentially the same teachings to the East that Christ later brought to the West. The central message of the Bhagavad Gita is that men and women may attain liberation through love for God, wisdom, and performance of right actions in the spirit of non-attachment. By dedicating all work to God and not identifying with the end results of our labors, we acknowledge that He is the doer not us. Thus Krishna said to his disciple Arjuna, "The God-united yogi, abandoning attachment to fruits of actions, attains the peace unshakable" (Bhagavad Gita V:12).

Even-Mindedness

Non-attachment leads to even-mindedness. "To be even-minded is to be always anchored in God. It is to live in His peace within as we pass through life — dealing effectively with every situation that arises, without becoming emotionally ruffled."[1] That is what Krishna meant when he said: "Be thou of even mind." Until we can deal with all dualities of the finite world such as war and peace, sickness and health, wealth and poverty and remain unaffected by them, we still have a major spiritual lesson to learn.

O, Arjuna! he who cannot be ruffled by these (contacts of the senses with their objects),
who is calm and evenminded during pain and pleasure, he alone is fit to attain everlastingness!
(Bhagavad Gita II:15).

On my most recent trip to India I was in Brindaban during the festival of Holi. Being in the midst of so many devoted village pilgrims was both uplifting and fun. They seemed to delight in tossing colored powders on everyone, including me. I noticed the children preferred to use the modern technology of squirt guns which

*Pilgrims to Brindaban during
Festival of Holi. Note purple powder
tossed in air in background.*

give them maximum range to spray their colored water. For me the day came to a close all too soon.

I left for Agra in the afternoon. Because of the huge volume of colored water tossed at rickshaws, my driver insisted on a circuitous route to avoid as many revellers as possible. We arrived in Agra in plenty of time for me to have dinner before taking an evening train.

Woman drying sari on banks of Yamuna River. Brindaban.

Great Mosque of Aurangzeb as seen from Ganges. Banaras.

The Holy City of Banaras

On my overnight coach to Banaras, I met two female students who were completing their last year of studies at Banaras University. Both planned to do social work after graduating. Prior to arriving in Banaras, I asked if it were appropriate to take them to dinner one evening. After discussing the matter in their own language, they accepted and a time was fixed.

When I went to meet them at their dormitory the next evening, they were outside waiting for me. I noticed a large group of young ladies standing nearby. They were residents of the dormitory who had assembled to see their two friends' "date." I was surprised that even though they were 21 years old, they had to be back at the dormitory for a 7:30 p.m. curfew for girls.

Banaras, the holiest and most beloved city of the Hindus, has been known by several names. The city once was called Kashi, but today it is known by its ancient Indian name Varanasi, which means "the city between two rivers." Built on the banks of the sacred Ganges, it is one of India's most important pilgrimage sites. It has been a center of learning for over 2,000 years. Located only six miles away is Sarnath, where Buddha preached his first sermon. To Hindus, Varanasi is considered an auspicious place to die.

Banaras' principal attraction is the continuous line of bathing *ghats* which are built on the west bank of the Ganges. There are over 100 *ghats* whose steps leading down to the river facilitate the pilgrims' performance of their ritual purification. Similarly, Christians are baptized in the River Jordan.

Dawn was approaching as I arrived at a bathing *ghat* from which I could hire a boat for an early morning ride on the Ganges. The trip was fascinating. The river's edge offered glimpses of many aspects of daily life. Some Hindus were performing rituals, while others were bathing or washing clothes.

What impressed me most about the many pilgrims was their devotion, which their facial expressions clearly mirrored. The cold morning air and water temperature did not chill their faith.

Monk sitting on steps of ghat after bath, applying religious markings to forehead. Banaras.

Golden Temple, Banaras.

Woman performing prayers in holy Ganges River. Banaras.

Early morning along Ganges. Note praying women holding lighted candles. Banaras.

Sunken temple, Ganges. Banaras.

Boat with pilgrims emerging from early morning fog on Ganges. Banaras.

Male pilgrims receiving prashad (divinely blessed sweets) from priest at ghat. Banaras.

Ghat, Banaras.

Male pilgrims bathing in Ganges.
Women on steps drying saris.
Banaras.

Uttar Pradesh

In the afternoon, I went to Durga Temple, commonly called the Monkey Temple due to the many monkeys who have made it their home. Before leaving for India, an American woman who previously had visited that country told me of a frightening incident. She had been chased by a band of vicious monkeys one afternoon when visiting a temple. She escaped by jumping onto a stone in a nearby stream and waiting there until the monkeys left. I accepted her fear into my consciousness, and hoped nothing like that would happen to me.

Fortunately, I was told another story about monkeys prior to my departure. It involved the early life of Swami Vivekananda, the chief disciple of the yogic master Sri Ramakrishna. When walking down a street of Banaras, he was followed by one monkey and then another. He became frightened, and the faster he walked, the more interested the monkeys became. The number increased until he was followed by a large troup. As he hurriedly rounded a corner trying to escape, he passed a *sadhu* sitting peacefully in meditation. Swami Vivekananda shouted to him, "What should I do?" The ascetic answered, "Face the brutes." He did, and the whole troup turned and fled. After hearing that story and realizing that monkeys were cowards, I no longer was afraid of them. As a result, I enjoyed all of my encounters with them — even the pesky ones. On several occasions I would playfully scold the aggressive ones for their unbecoming behavior, and invariably they turned and went away.

Sarnath

Early the next morning, I went to Sarnath. It was there at the Deer Park that the Buddha preached his first sermon to his fellow ascetics after having become enlightened at Bodh Gaya.

The excavations at Sarnath are extensive. In addition to a large restored *stupa* believed to date from about 500 A.D., the ruins include foundations of many early Buddhist buildings which are over 1,500 years old. Two Chinese travelers who visited the site in 640 A.D. recorded that the colony had over 1,500 priests and a *stupa* nearly 300 feet high. They also saw an imposing pillar over 60 feet high, erected by Ashoka, the great emperor and patron of Buddhism. The famous lion capital from the remnants of the Ashokan pillar, circa 250 B.C., is still in pristine condition. The highly polished fluted capital may be seen in the local museum. The Ashokan symbol of four back-to-back lions is the symbol of modern India.

Sarnath's excellent Archaeological Museum also contains perhaps the most sublime example of Gupta sculpture. The magnificently carved fifth century A.D. sandstone Buddha is seated as a yogi on a throne. His hands perform a *mudra* (formal gesture), symbolizing that he is preaching the Buddhist Law. His upper body is backed by a huge intricately decorated halo with two heavenly beings flying at the top.

Buddhism already was in decline when the destructive Muslim invasions began. Sarnath was not spared. Its buildings were destroyed and desecrated. Even the usually tolerant Akbar built a monument to his father over one of the *stupas*.

As sunset approached, I returned to Banaras. The peaceful feeling I experienced at Sarnath was so strong that I made a vow to visit the Buddha's birthplace in present-day Nepal. It was then that I realized one of my purposes for coming to India — to receive the vibrations of the Great Ones.

Prayer flags. Site of the Buddha's first sermon. Sarnath.

Seated Buddha preaching the Law. Gupta Dynasty, 5th century. Archaeological Museum, Sarnath.

Portion of estimated 19 million pilgrims who bathed in river during auspicious 24 hour period. Kumbha Mela, Allahabad.

The Kumbha Mela at Allahabad

The *Kumbha Mela* represents the heart and soul of India. For thousands of years, saints and sages have come from the Himalayan Mountains and forests to attend this ancient festival, thereby keeping spiritual goals in constant sight of the ordinary person. Tens of millions of devout Hindus gather here every 12 years to purify themselves in the Ganges River and to mingle with the thousands of *sadhus*, yogis, swamis and ascetics of all types. Many are hermits who leave their secluded abodes only to attend the *melas*, where they bestow their blessings upon the multitudes. There are many impostors and hypocrites, but "For the faults of the many, judge not the whole. Everything on earth is of mixed character.... Though many *sadhus* here still wander in delusion, yet the *mela* is blessed by a few men of God-realization."[2]

The site of the gathering at Allahabad is the vast expanse of land located on both sides of two of India's most important rivers — the Ganges and Yamuna. Hindus believe bathing at the *sangam*, the confluence, gives special purification. The *sangam* is thought to be made even more sacred by the merging of a third river, the invisible heavenly or astral Saraswati.

On the Yamuna side of the confluence stands a historic fort built by Akbar in 1583. Allahabad also was the site where the British East India Company officially ceded control over India to the British government in 1858, following the Indian Mutiny.

The *Kumbha Mela* is the largest religious festival in the world. It lasts from mid-January to mid-February, and on auspicious astrological days, the surging crowds swell to over 19 million! It was on one of those four special days that I arrived. As I neared the grounds, thousands of people were entering and leaving.

Kumbha Mela, Allahabad, Uttar Pradesh

My rickshaw driver insisted on dropping me at the main gate to avoid having to deal with the congestion inside. I was now on my own to find a small plot of land which was the camp where I would be staying. My home for the next three days was surrounded by an ocean of humanity, and I had forgotten to bring its plot designation with me! I began walking with the flow of pedestrians not knowing where I was going. I passed through the arch of a large wooden gate, marking the formal entrance to the *mela's* grounds. A thrill went through me as I thought of all the sacred feet which had trod this path before me. Although it took me about three hours to find my camp, I was grateful to have arrived at all.

After having a simple dinner, I toured the grounds and visited other *ashrams*. One organization had neon displays of scenes from the scriptures. The one that got the most attention was a god shooting an arrow whose trajectory found its mark in the chest of a villain. Though the lectures at our camp were given in Hindi, someone translated parts of them for me. One of the points that impressed me was: "Life is a school. Do not look for happiness here. It will come later." Said another way, "The things that happen to us do not matter; what we become through them does."[3] When I asked the monk later to elaborate on what he meant, he replied, "If we become ruffled, remember that it is God who is arranging those circumstances to show us our ego." I think all religions agree that "When the 'I' shall die, then shall I know who am I."

Because of snows in the Himalayas, the nights were extremely cold. I bought an extra wool blanket and slept in my warmest clothes. I noticed some peasants sleeping on the ground in lightweight clothing. Many had only cotton blankets and some had no coverings at all. Devotion!

The camp directly across from ours used a loudspeaker at an ear-piercing volume. The speaker system blared 15 to 17 hours a day, as various persons of all ages evidently gave testimonials praising God. When a Westerner complained about the noise to an Indian, he responded: "If you understood what they are saying, you would not say that." From that moment, I had a new attitude towards the noise produced by so many people.

That afternoon, I was invited to join a group who hired a large boat to go to the *sangam* (confluence) to bathe. There were hundreds of similar boats ferrying pilgrims to the auspicious spot. Several Hindus wished me well while I was in the water, and appreciated my honoring their rituals. I was unable to see the banks because of the vast numbers of bathers.

Parade of sadhus en route to river to bathe. Kumbha Mela, Allahabad.

Pilgrims in boat at confluence of Yamuna and Ganges rivers, the most auspicious spot to bathe. Kumbha Mela, Allahabad.

Kumbha Mela grounds become a tent city. Early morning, Allahabad.

Ascetic with ashes smeared on body. He has renounced material possessions in quest for God. Kumbha Mela.

Opposite ▷
Shrine commemorating Paramahansa Yogananda at Yogoda Satsanga camp. Kumbha Mela, Allahabad.

Visiting the *Kumbha Mela* was especially memorable. It helped me to pierce the shroud of that country's mystique, and to intimately witness its outpouring of devotion.

Aarti. Har ki Pairi ghat. Hardwar.

Abstract image of a deity, Mansa Devi Temple. Hardwar.

Hardwar: "Gateway to Heaven"

Hardwar is one of my favorite places in all of India. Located in the foothills of the Himalayas where the Ganges begins its flow across the plains, it can be reached from Delhi in only six hours by bus or a little longer by overnight train. No trip to India is complete without visiting Hardwar's Har ki Pairi *ghat* in the evening. Hundreds of pilgrims sing evening prayers while priests on the opposite bank wave flaming lamps (*aarti*). Many of them release small "leaf boats" containing flowers and a lighted candle into the swiftly flowing river. I loved the inspiring *aarti* ceremony so much that I went to Hardwar often.

Pilgrims, Har ki Pairi ghat. Hardwar.

*Priests with flaming lamps performing aarti. Har ki Pairi ghat.
Hardwar.*

*Flower seller, Har ki Pairi ghat.
Hardwar.*

*Woman placing flower
offering with lighted
candle in Ganges. Har
ki Pairi ghat.
Hardwar.*

Mt. Meru, source of Ganges River. Garhwal Himalayan Mountains, Gangotri region.

Yamunotri, Gangotri, Kedarnath and Badrinath

Located northeast of Rishikesh in an area known as the Garhwal Himalayas are four sacred Hindu pilgrimage sites. Yamunotri is at the source of the Yamuna River and Gangotri is near the glacial origin of the Ganges at Gaumukh. The mountaintop temple at Kedarnath is located at an altitude of 11,750 feet. It is situated at the base of an impressive snow covered peak. From the town below, the temple can only be reached by foot, horseback or by being carried up the steep terrain in a chair supported on the shoulders of four men. Badrinath is dedicated to Lord Vishnu and is accessible by car or bus. Near Badrinath is Joshimath, where there is a sacred cave once used by the philosopher-saint Shankara when he journeyed to Badrinath on foot in the eighth century.

To visit the four remote Himalayan pilgrimage sites, I took a bus tour organized by the Uttar Pradesh Tourist Bureau which lasted 12 days. I was the only foreigner on the pilgrimage. The group of about 20 Hindus "adopted" me, and made sure that I was as comfortable as the rustic circumstances allowed. Each morning immediately before the bus began the day's journey, they would shout in unison an affirmation to God. It was very inspiring.

The night before we made the trip to Kedarnath, the women prepared a special meal. Because it was raining, I had on old clothes. To my embarrassment when I entered the small kitchen to eat, all of the women had on fine saris. They had brought them especially for this occasion to honor God on the evening before our sacred ascent. It is said that all who make the pilgrimage to Kedarnath and Badrinath will be brother and sister disciples for life.

To make the pilgrimage is an act of faith. The narrow mountain roads are so dangerous that I am surprised there are not more collisions involving buses. Our driver was excellent, although I cannot say the same for the others. Because of snow and monsoon rains, roads are only open during the summer and early fall. On my trip, which was during the end of the monsoon in mid-September, a landslide prevented us from reaching Yamunotri. The rains made the mountains lush and green.

Overleaf ▷
Local people bathing on holy day at confluence of Bhagirathi and Alaknanda rivers, the point where Ganges River gets its name. Denprayag, Garhwal Himalayas.

Mt. Shivling, 21,000 feet high, is both the mythological and physical source of the Ganges River. Garhwal Himalayan Mountains, Gangotri region.

Monsoon season, Garhwal Himalayan Mountains.

Badrinath Temple.

Kedarnath Temple.

Woman with children. Dwarahat.

Women carrying fodder. Dwarahat.

Dwarahat

About 100 miles south of Badrinath is the small Himalayan town of Dwarahat. I was making a pilgrimage to a cave once inhabited by an Indian *avatar* known as Babaji (Reverend Father).

It was cold and dark when I finally arrived at my destination, a small *ashram* built on a hill outside of Dwarahat. The next morning after a simple breakfast, a monk from the *ashram* led me to the cave.

When we returned, the monk told me some parables. Several of the allegories were from the *shastras* ("sacred books") and contained profound truths under a veil of detailed symbolism from the <u>Puranas</u>. They related to the importance of keeping one's word. The following story had a deep impact on me.[4]

Once a beautiful pigeon pursued by a hawk dropped from the sky and sought protection from the king of Banaras. Seeing the pigeon's terror, the king said, "Be comforted, good bird. Fear not; for none need fear who seek protection here. For thy protection I will surrender all my kingdom; yea if need be, life itself."

The hawk challenged the king's words and said, "This bird is my appointed food. Thou shouldst not protect my lawful prey, won by hard endeavor. O king, hunger is gnawing at my stomach. Thou hast the right to intervene when human beings fight; but what lawful power hast thou over the birds that range the sky?" Then the king said: "So be it; let a bull or boar or deer be dressed for thee, for thou shalt not have the bird." But the hawk replied: "I do not eat the flesh of bulls or boars or deer. Pigeons are my appointed food. But if thou hast such affection for the pigeon, give flesh from thine own body equal to the pigeon's weight." The king agreed and the pigeon was placed in one of the pans of a scale.

As the king began cutting off strips of his flesh, the earth shook to bear witness to his act of keeping his word. Though the king cut flesh from his arms and thighs, he filled the scale in vain; for the gods caused the pigeon to weigh heavier than the flesh. Even after stripping away all of his flesh, the scale would not budge. When the king was nothing but a skeleton, he desired to give his whole body, and stepped into the scale. Then the gods appeared, and for his joyful sacrifice to defend the weak and unprotected, they restored his body and took him away to heaven.

The story has several morals: The importance of keeping one's word; it is the duty of the strong to protect the weak; and God can give us some harsh tests until we prove ourselves worthy. In other words, our belief in God must be tested to prove its value.

One of Shakespeare's most well-known plays, <u>The Merchant of Venice</u>, has a similar plot which requires a merchant to forfeit a pound of flesh for his failure to fulfill the terms of a financial contract. It is interesting to note that the play's primary message — the importance of keeping one's word — has been overlooked in favor of lesser themes.

Throughout the ages, the ideal of truth (*satya*) has permeated Hindu society. Its scriptures proclaim that those who habitually speak only the truth develop the power of materializing their words. "What commands they utter from the heart come to pass" (<u>Yoga Sutras</u> II:36). Marco Polo said of his travels to India, that the priests "would not utter a lie for anything on earth." In the annals of English judges and administrators during the British Colonial Period, one judge wrote, "I have had before me hundreds of cases in which a man's property, liberty, or life depended on his telling a lie; and he has refused to tell it."

Jammu and Kashmir

The Mountain Paradise of Kashmir

Many travelers think Kashmir is the most beautiful region in the world. Its green valleys and beautiful lakes, serenely guarded by the snow-capped Himalayas, have earned it the name of "Little Switzerland." As I stepped off the plane and inhaled a deep breath of refreshing mountain air, I understood why its cool climate has long made it a retreat from the heat of the Indian plains. I was looking forward to a much needed rest.

Srinagar

Srinagar, the capital of Kashmir, was founded in the third century B.C. by Emperor Ashoka. He constructed 500 monasteries there, of which 100 still stood 1,000 years later.

The city is built on Dal Lake, and is the scenic state's greatest attraction. Portions of the lake are afloat with houseboats, where one can sit on a veranda and forget the worries of the world.

The houseboats were the ingenious idea of the British, who were not allowed to own land there during the Raj period. My houseboat consisted of a Victorian living room, a dining room, and two bedrooms, each with modern Western bathrooms. The owner, Mohammed, lived in an adjacent houseboat. Every morning, he would ask me what foods and fresh vegetables I would like prepared for my meals. After I got to know him better, he invited me to eat breakfast with his family, but preferred to serve me lunch and dinner in my more luxurious quarters.

Houseboats on Dal Lake, Srinagar, Kashmir.

*Vegetable sellers in shikara (boat) on
Dal Lake. Srinagar.*

*Young Muslim girl sitting on dock.
Dal Lake. Srinagar.*

Houseboats, Dal Lake. Srinagar.

Roses, Dal Lake. Srinagar.

Srinagar, Jammu and Kashmir

Man poling shikara loaded with roots harvested from Dal Lake.

One of the more enjoyable experiences in Srinagar is riding through the maze of peaceful waterways on a *shikara*, one of the long, graceful boats which ply the lakes. A deluxe *shikara* has a canopy and thick-cushioned "full spring seats" which make the leisurely trip comfortable.

The Mughal rulers of India also appreciated Kashmir. Akbar built a fort on a hill overlooking the city and it makes a scenic backdrop. Formal gardens whose style was refined to an art by the Mughal kings are well maintained. Shalimar Gardens, originally built by Jehangir for his wife, was filled with some of the most beautiful roses I have ever seen. For a small tip, the gardeners delighted in cutting whichever ones the Indian tourists wanted.

Kashmir's predominantly Muslim population would prefer to be independent from India. Some would like to become a part of Pakistan.

Kashmir was not originally a part of British India. It was a princely state, whose ruler chose what country he would join. L. Collins and D. Lapierre's <u>Freedom at Midnight</u> relates how the Maharaja's indecisive action led to a Pakistani invasion which resulted in the first Indo-Pakistan conflict. The region is now divided with approximately two-thirds belonging to India and one-third to Pakistan, but both countries claim it all.

The current political turmoil in Kashmir is symptomatic of India's tremendous challenge to keep the nation from fragmenting. Many minority cultures in India want to establish their own independent countries, claiming they were once separate political units. Such arguments are clearly untenable to the Indian central government. Indians of different religions and ethnic groups will just have to learn to get along with each other! The creation of the modern states of Pakistan and India have proven that separating people by religion is not the solution to global peace.

Sixty miles from Srinagar is the town of Pahalgam. It is built on the narrow, fast flowing Lidder River whose blue green water is filled with moss laden boulders. I stayed at a hotel which was so near the river that its rushing waters lulled me to sleep at night. What a pleasure it was to awake each morning greeted by the river's salutation. The early morning sunlight illuminated the fir-covered, snow-capped mountains which were silhouetted against a blue sky. The Cosmic Artist was at it again!

The mountain air was so invigorating that I decided to hike to some nearby towns. Loading a small back pack with as few necessities as possible, I walked about eight miles along the Lidder River to the little village of Aru. There I spent the night and continued on the next day to Lidderwat. My four hour hike took me through spectacular mountain scenery. Many shepherds had brought their flocks of sheep to the high meadows for the summer.

After returning to Srinagar, I took a bus to Gulmarg, located less than 35 miles away. Situated at an altitude of over 8,200 feet, it gets extremely cold at night. "Gulmarg" means "meadow of flowers," and I was told that in the spring, it truly is that. The small valley was ringed by intimidating mountains, giving the impression that one was a prisoner of nature.

My hotel was on a steep hill. The lushness of the valley's rolling green hills gave the appearance of springtime. A dense forest growing on the side of the mountain was partially shrouded by mist. Floating clusters of white clouds concealed patches of the tall timbered sentinels higher up the precipice. Above the clouds the trees reappeared, forming an abrupt contrast to the dark, barren, snow-capped bluffs higher up. Frozen rivers of snow extending down the slopes would thaw later on, and send water to the valley below. Light and dark clouds concealed the setting sun, providing celestial back-lighting for the magnificent view. It seemed a shame that nature's tranquility could not be shared by its human inhabitants.

Mosque in Himalayan Mountains. Gulmarg.

Ladakh

Averaging 20,000 to 23,000 feet high, the towering Karakoram Mountain range allows less than 4 inches of rain per year. Ladakh.

Buddhist monks chanting prayers during ceremony. Tikse Gompa, Ladakh.

Ladakh

I had heard so many exotic stories about Ladakh from travelers that I was eager to visit the old kingdom. Ladakh is about the size of England and is located high in the Himalayan Mountains due east of and contiguous with Kashmir. The area often is called "Little Tibet." Its people, culture and Tantric Buddhist religion and monasteries are a microcosm of what Tibet was like before the Chinese invaded.

Ladakh has one of the highest elevations of any inhabited region in the world. It also has one of the most arid climates, as the colossal Karakoram Mountains allow less than four inches of rainfall annually. Most of its elevated mountains are completely devoid of plant life, which prompts many travelers to compare the rugged terrain to the barren landscape of the moon. Isolated from the rest of the world for about eight months a year, Ladakh's high plateau could be "Shangri-la" from the movie *Lost Horizons*.

Ladakh is part of the modern Indian state of Jammu and Kashmir which is predominantly Muslim with its capital in Srinagar. The 45,000 square miles of Ladakhi desert constitute the greater part of the region. The Buddhist majority of Ladakh want to be formally separated from the pro-Muslim government. To further complicate the political situation, the Chinese invaded Ladakh in 1962, and today the Sino-Indian border remains a tense militarized zone.

The overland route from Srinagar to Leh takes two 12 hour days, but the towering passes are only open to vehicles from late May to October. My 30 minute flight from Srinagar over the snow-covered mountain peaks was impressive. The airport is located on a hilltop overlooking the Indus River. At the end of the runway, the 1,000 year old Spitok Gompa (monastery) welcomes travelers to another world.

It is only a short jeep ride from the airport into the small city of Ley, which has a population of about 25,000. On a mountainside overlooking the town is Leh Palace.

Early one morning, I hiked up to the old palace. When I arrived, a Ladakhi man met me and unlocked the door to the library. Large carvings of Buddhas and *Bodhisattvas* (saints) peered at me from the shadows. Columns supporting the ceiling were painted with vivid Tantric Buddhist motifs. Old carved wooden dance masks worn by monks in allegorical plays hung from them. Some depicted horned animals with their supernatural powers; others had fierce looking human faces with the spiritual eye marked at the forehead. They represented benevolent spirits who possessed tremendous prowess to ward off evil spirits.

Located higher up the mountain was a simply constructed monastery over 550 years old. Inside was a giant seated Buddha, three stories high. From the monastery, there was a splendid view of the Indus Valley. The river sustained a green strip of vegetation on either side, which disappeared into the dust of the barren hills. Because I was not acclimated to the high altitudes, I had to stop several times during my climb to catch my breath. It is not uncommon for visitors to Ley to have splitting headaches for the first 24 hours until their bodies readjust to an altitude of over 10,500 feet, and I was no exception.

Carved wooden animal mask, 19th century. Leh Palace, Ladakh.

Tikse Gompa, Ladakh.

Carved wooden Buddha, two stories high, is said to be one of the most important statues in Ladakh. Alchi Gompa.

Tikse Gompa (monastery), near Ley, Ladakh.

Located about 10 miles from Ley is Tikse Gompa. Its numerous white-washed buildings sprawl down the side of a barren, rocky mountain.

The path winding up the steep hill to the Tikse monastery did not look intimidating, but because of the low oxygen content at that altitude, it took me much longer to climb than I had anticipated. No clouds shielded the bright sun, and I was glad that I had a canteen of water with me.

When I reached the top, much to my delight, a Buddhist ceremony was in progress. Many of the monks were gathered in a courtyard. The old monk, whom I assume was in charge of the monastery, was wearing a crown and ceremonial robe. He was sitting in front of a fire, which probably symbolized the purifying flames which destroy one's *karma*. He was holding a prayer bell in his left hand which he rang periodically, and with two fingers of his right hand he occasionally dropped a powdered substance into the fire, which caused bright bursts of flames to shoot upwards.

Buddhist monk conducting ceremony. Tikse Gompa, Ladakh.

India Unveiled   117

Indus River, near Ley. Ladakh.

Buddhist monks sitting in monastery courtyard. One is holding mirror while shaving. Sumur, Nubra Valley, Ladakh.

Several days later when walking across a field near the Indus River en route to a cave temple, I came upon a huge pile of *mani* stones, each beautifully carved. Inscribed on them was *Om mani padme hum*. The famous Tibetan mantra literally means "Praise to the Jewel at the Heart of the Lotus." Its metaphysical significance affirms the brilliance of God's illumining light at the spiritual eye between the eyebrows. Evidently, the *mani* stones had been placed there by individuals making a pilgrimage to the same cave.

Mani stones in field overlooking Indus River. Near Ley.

dakhi children. Khardung, Nubra Valley.

Hemis Gompa, Ladakh

About 25 miles from Ley is Hemis Gompa, one of the largest and most important monasteries in Ladakh. It would be easy to pass by this monastery if one did not know of its location because it is tucked under the summit of a steep mountain. Site of the most famous *gompa* festival in Ladakh, it has many well-preserved wall paintings. I was eager to visit the library with its ancient manuscripts, and the monk showing me around unlocked it for me. It was at Hemis in 1887 that the Russian traveler Nicholas Notovitch persuaded a monk to show him the two books, which according to Buddhist accounts recorded Jesus Christ's visit to India. The document covers Jesus' life from age 13 to 26, the major portion of his missing years not accounted for in the Bible. The chronicle confirms that Jesus visited the famous Indian sites of the Jagannath Temple in Puri and other such sacred cities as Banaras. Some believe that Jesus' trip to India was to return the visit of the "three wise men from the East" who came to Bethlehem to honor His arrival on earth.

Aided by his interpreter who translated from the Tibetan language, Notovitch carefully wrote down the various verses as they were read to him. Published in 1894 as <u>The Unknown Life of Jesus Christ</u>, the account is available in English (translated from the French by V. R. Gandhi) for all who may wish to determine its validity. Notovitch never doubted the document's authenticity and showed his translation to leading European ecclesiastics and a cardinal connected with the Vatican to get their opinions. All tried to dissuade him from making public his discovery.

The early Buddhist account of Jesus' life and death vindicated the Sanhedrin, whom by the Roman governor's order summoned Jesus to appear before the tribunal. The Buddhist chronicle portrays sympathy between the elders of Israel and Jesus, and their findings sent to Pilate were: "We will not judge a just man." According to Notovitch, the Buddhist document makes clear that Pilate alone was responsible for Jesus' death, not the Pharisees and the Jews. Pilate viewed Jesus' growing popularity as a threat to himself and to Rome's control over the ancient Jewish nation, and he manipulated a scenario to have Jesus put to death.

Buddhist monk holding key to library. Old manuscripts are kept in boxes and wrapped in cloth. Hemis Gompa, Ladakh.

Buddhist statuary, Hemis Gompa.

Giant thangka (religious painting) unfurled from roof of Lekir Gompa. It is said to be displayed only for special holidays which occur 8 to 12 years apart. Ladakh.

The Ladakhis are a warm and friendly people. Anyone who has ever visited there will remember the big smiles and rosy cheeks when greeted with their traditional welcome *"Jullay."* Monasteries laden with paintings and art objects place Ladakh high on my list of the world's most exotic places to visit.

The Golden Temple of Amritsar

The holy city of Amritsar, the Sikhs' Mecca, was founded in 1577 and is only 16 miles from the border of Pakistan. The Golden Temple, the Sikhs' holiest shrine, is located there. The city was sacked by a Mughal emperor in 1761 and the temple was destroyed. It was rebuilt in 1764, and in 1802 the roof was covered with gilded copper plates. Ever since, it has been known as "the Golden Temple."

The two story marble temple sits regally in a large, sacred pool from which Amritsar (Pool of Immortality-giving Nectar) received its name. The temple is a blend of Hindu and Muslim architectural styles and is reached by a marble causeway known as Gurus' Bridge.

Sikh pilgrim standing in front of the Golden Temple. Amritsar.

Priest reading from original copy of Granth Sahib, the Sikh's holy book. Golden Temple. Amritsar.

I covered my head and washed my feet in the wading pool, as all are required to do. Crossing the crowded, narrow causeway, I entered the temple. Inside, a priest was reading from the original copy of the Sikhs' holy book, the Granth Sahib, which contained the tenets from the 10 Sikh gurus as well as Hindu and Muslim writings. The readings and singings of the hymns are broadcast by loudspeakers and resonate within the walls of the huge compound. A male singer was accompanied by a harmonium, my favorite Indian instrument. I found the chanting so uplifting that one afternoon I sat on the upper floor of the temple and listened to the enrapturing music for hours.

About 10:00 p.m. each evening, the holy book is ceremoniously returned to the Parliament building, located within the vast complex. Once the scripture is removed from the temple and carried across the causeway, it is placed in a box on a palanquin and is transported the short distance to where it is stored overnight. There it remains until early the next morning, when it is again reverently returned to the temple. The Sikhs' fervor on the night I remained for the processional was similar to that of Jews when the Torah is removed from the Ark and paraded through the synagogue. After the ceremony was over, we were all given *prashad* (ritually blessed sweets).

Sikh men attending evening prayers. Golden Temple, upper floor. Amritsar.

The Sikh religion was founded in 1469 by the God-realized Guru Nanak, who was revered by both Hindus and Muslims. He espoused the best of both religions and made a conscious attempt to harmonize the two most powerful rival religions of India. To this day, Guru Nanak is venerated by Sikhs, Hindus and Muslims, and offers an enduring testimonial to the power of divine love.

One of the concepts of the Sikhs is *Guru Ka Langar* (common kitchen), which was established to abolish caste distinction. Nearly all Sikh temples have a community kitchen where volunteers prepare free meals for pilgrims. At the Golden Temple in Amritsar, thousands of people are fed daily. The large dining hall was filled with long rows of pilgrims sitting on straw mats in the customary Indian manner. I enjoyed the simple meal of *chapatis* and lentils on several occasions. Sikh temples also provide free accommodations to all at *gurdwaras* (guest houses) which are located nearby.

In an attempt to halt Muslim persecution and atrocities, military overtones were introduced into the Sikh religion during the 17th century. Several of the Sikh gurus transformed their followers into a formidable military force which successfully fought the Mughal Islamic rulers of India. It was the last Sikh guru, Guru Govind Singh (1675-1708), who founded the *Khalsa*, the militant Sikh theocracy. He required all Sikhs to assume the surname Singh, meaning "Lion," so they might be united to fight the religiously intolerant Mughals. Since that time, most of the Sikhs have assumed the surname Singh, although having that name does not necessarily mean that one is a Sikh; many Rajputs have the same name.

The Sikhs place great emphasis on the work ethic. As a result of their toil, the Punjab is the most developed agricultural state in India today, and its per capita income is nearly double India's average. These successes can be largely attributed to their industriousness, as other areas of India have land as fertile.

When leaving Amritsar by train, I met a young Sikh college graduate who wanted to become a jet pilot in the Indian Air Force. He informed me that many young Sikhs like himself violated religious prohibitions and trimmed their beards and cut their hair, even though it could not be seen under their turbans. He explained that it was their way of identifying with the modern world.

Politically, the Punjab is highly volatile as religious separatists insist on their own country. They submitted a charter of demands which the Indian central government did not accept. In the early 1980s, Sikh terrorists occupied the Golden Temple, and were finally evicted in 1984 by the Indian army when no compromise could be reached. The numerous deaths resulting from the army's bloody assault on the temple led to the assassination of Prime Minister Indira Gandhi in 1984 by her Sikh bodyguards. Though the political differences in the Punjab still remain unresolved, religious issues seem to play a very minor part. Most of the Sikhs whom I met were glad that the insurgency involving the Golden Temple was over. I left the Punjab with renewed hope for a harmonious India.

Sikhs in contemplation. Golden Temple. Amritsar.

Religious pictures with electric lights, primarily of Sikh gurus. Shop owner wearing blue turban is reflected in mirror. Amritsar.

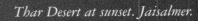
Thar Desert at sunset. Jaisalmer.

Chapter Four

Rajasthan

◁ Opposite Women admiring Jain sculpture. Ranakpur temple.

The Northwest: A Sojourn to Exotic Rajasthan

Rajasthan was the home of the Rajputs, a group of warrior clans who controlled that part of northwest India for a thousand years. Their codes of conduct, chivalry and honor were similar to the knights of medieval Europe. Like the warring city-states of Northern Italy, the Rajputs, when not fighting outsiders, were quarreling with each other; thus, they never became a united force and were no match for the invading Mughals. But their bravery, honor, loyalty and love of freedom have remained a legendary inspiration without parallel in the annals of most nations.

Rajput warriors seldom surrendered regardless of the size of the invading army. When defeat was inevitable, the women and children committed suicide by marching into a funeral pyre in a ritual known as *jauhar*. The men, dressed not in armor but in holy saffron robes, rode off to certain death. Time and time again in Rajput history, they chose the honor of death rather than surrender. It was not uncommon for tens of thousands of warriors to die this way in battle.

I met a member of the *Kshtriya* (warrior) caste who told me that his father taught him only two things could stop a *Kshtriya* from succeeding: God and death. From his mother, he learned never to start something unless he completed it, and whatever he did, he should do from the heart. The noble Rajput legacy stirs my soul and always adds to the thrill of traveling in Rajasthan. Their courage and valor have become part of the heritage of modern India.

City Palace. Udaipur. Largest palace complex in Rajasthan.

Udaipur

I thought Udaipur was the most beautiful city in India. It is built around lovely Pichola Lake. Palaces perched on rugged mountains formed a picturesque backdrop. Most of Udaipur's houses and palaces are painted white, which reminded me of the splendor of Greek islands such as Mykonos. They present a handsome contrast to the blue lake and arid landscape.

Udaipur was founded in 1567, and has several famous palaces. The huge City Palace dominates the lake, and is the largest complex in Rajasthan. It is a conglomeration of buildings, added over hundreds of years by various rulers, yet it retains a remarkable stylistic uniformity with its uniquely Indian gates, arches, towers and cupolas. The Lake Palace, built in 1754, entirely covers a small island and has been converted into a luxury hotel.

I hired a motor rickshaw to tour the city, which enabled me to stay as long as I wished at several of its excellent museums. I was impressed by the grandeur of the City Palace, which is the residence of the line of Maharajas who formerly ruled the princely state. It is one of India's most spectacular palaces with its brightly colored mosaics of peacocks, the favorite Rajasthani bird. The palace is known for its gracefully carved arches and 18th and 19th century Indian miniatures and paintings. The tiger hunting scenes from the Maharaja period of British Colonialism depicted royal parties in regal howdahs riding on top of elephants.

Stained glass. Throne room, City Palace. Udaipur.

Royal elephant. Wall painting, City Palace. Udaipur.

Guards sitting in interior courtyard.
City Palace. Udaipur.

Ranakpur

One morning I took a tour to Ranakpur, the largest Jain temple in India. The two story structure, built in 1439, had many towers rising from its roof. Inside, 29 halls were supported by 1,944 pillars, no two alike. One of the intricately carved pillars was purposely erected at an angle. The deliberate error symbolized the imperfection of humankind.

Worshipers standing before altar. Jain temple, Ranakpur.

Jain temple. Ranakpur.

Sculptural detail, Jain temple. Ranakpur.

Marble dome, Jain temple. Ranakpur.

Because of his reverence for all life, Orthodox Jain priest wears scarf over his nose to keep from breathing in insects. Jain temple. Ranakpur.

Rishabhanatha, also known as Adinatha, the first Jain saint. Jain temple. Ranakpur.

Hawa Mahal, Palace of the Winds. Jaipur.

Jaipur

Jaipur is the capital city of the state of Rajasthan, and has a population of over 1,500,000. It derived its name of the "pink city" from the pink painted buildings which line the streets of its old walled city. It is not known when the tradition of painting its edifices pink began. Some say that it was initiated in 1876 to honor the visit of the Prince of Wales, who later became King Edward VII.

Jaipur's central landmark is the Hawa Mahal (Palace of the Winds). It is located in the old city and was built in 1799. The unusual five story building is actually little more than a facade. It was built to enable ladies of the royal household to observe everyday life along the city streets without being seen. Carved stone lattice screens, which become more intricate with each successive story, cover every window.

From a rooftop vantage point at the local silver market, I watched an endless procession of people. Many of the women wore colorful Rajasthani clothing and the men had on pastel turbans. The old city's broad avenues and spacious bazaars were modeled after European cities.

Many cows were present on the sidewalks, and occasionally one would walk into the streets, bringing an abrupt halt to rush hour traffic. Usually someone would good-naturedly shoo the animal out of the way, but sometimes the sacred bovine received a not so propitious whack on the flanks with a long stick. Pedestrians shared the wide sidewalks with the cows, walking around them whenever one blocked the way. The coexistence of people and animals in the midst of a bustling city was a sight not to be seen in the West.

In addition to the usual vehicles which filled the crowded streets, Jaipur had an unusual mode of conveyance. Strange-looking camel-drawn carts combined modern technology with the ancient world. They rolled along at a surprisingly fast pace on two rubber automobile tires.

A maze of small alleys intersected the broad avenues of the old city. While wandering through them, I bought savory foods from several street vendors. Most Westerners I met would not eat food sold on the streets, but vegetarian foods are usually safe, provided they are obtained immediately upon coming from the boiling oil.

The famous fortress-palace of Amber is located seven miles from Jaipur and was the ancient capital of the old state of Jaipur. Construction was begun in 1592 by the Rajput commander whom Akbar the Great, the enlightened Mughal Emperor of India, selected as head of his armies.

Situated on a hillside and surrounded by walls, the citadel commands an imposing view of the neighboring mountains. To visit the maharaja's apartments on the upper level, I passed through the beautiful Hall of Victory, with its unusual damascene wall panels.

Overhead on the ceiling, mirrors glimmered from the sun. At the end of the open hall, there was an impressive view of the countryside, where protective walls traversed the barren mountains for great distances, resembling a smaller version of the Great Wall of China.

Street scene, old city in late afternoon. Jaipur.

Jaipur, Rajasthan

City Palace. Jaipur.

Street vendor selling peas. Jaipur.

Amber Palace. Jaipur environs. Begun 1592.

Meherangarh Fort. Jodhpur.

Jodhpur

We arrived in Jodhpur early in the morning. When I went to the old part of the city, it was like stepping into a fairy tale. The men were wearing colorful turbans and had full moustaches which curled at each end. The women were dressed in bright fabrics, and they looked like images from travel posters. A fort located on a high hill dominated the view. Rocky cliffs provided an impenetrable barrier from several directions, making it the most formidable citadel in the "Land of the Kings."

A winding road led up to the Jodhpur fort from the city below. The luxuriously decorated palace is still owned by the Maharaja of Jodhpur. I hired a guide to learn more about the history of the fort. He was wearing a red turban and handsomely dressed in a white tunic with a red sash around his waist.

After passing through a series of gates, I noticed small hand prints set into the wall. The hand prints, or *sati* marks, belonged to Maharaja Man Singh's widows, who in 1843 threw themselves upon his funeral pyre to be true to their vows. A garland of flowers had been placed around them, commemorating the women's bravery and turning the wall into a shrine.

As a result of the Hindu matrimonial tradition of the wife totally surrendering her will to her husband, a very strong bond of harmony often developed between them. At her husband's death, when she felt she could not go on living without him, she would throw herself upon his funeral pyre. The practice was known as *sati*, and in its very early days it was an uncoerced act of love and loyalty.

*Hand prints (sati marks) of
Maharaja Man Singh's widows
who threw themselves upon his
funeral pyre in 1843.
Meherangarh Fort. Jodhpur.*

Though *sati* originally was optional, it later was carried out by force. If a woman refused to enter her husband's funeral pyre, she often was burned alive with him by his relatives to maintain the family's honor.

The British put an end to the custom by banning it. It had become a socially degrading act which tied a woman's destiny to that of her husband, when her ultimate allegiance should be to God and not to man.

Sati also opens the question of the denial of widows' rights to remarry, which was not a part of the Hindu custom. Even in extreme circumstances in child marriages when the husband died early, she could not remarry. Today a Hindu widow can remarry, but there is still social stigma connected with it.

Historically, there were two grounds on which a woman in Rajasthan might take her own life: by *jauhar* or by *sati*. Because a *Kshatriya* (caste) warrior could enforce a marriage on his captive without her consent, Rajput women often chose to march into a funeral pyre to maintain their honor and to preserve the social custom of being married to only one man during their lifetime. This ritual known as *jauhar* was not a social evil, but had merit. The woman immolated herself for modesty. She was not forced into that action by anyone.

Sati, when performed voluntarily as an act of devotion, also had merit. It illustrated the wife's unconditional love and loyalty to her husband. It was her ultimate gift — the giving of her self — even if it represented the limited understanding that existed during the Middle Ages.

Such drastic measures as *sati* or the extreme flagellations performed by certain Catholic saints to overcome the ego are no longer needed in this higher age. We now understand the science of yoga and the purpose of ultimate fulfillment: to unite our souls with God. Today, greater spiritual perspective and yogic methods to obtain that union are available. Thus, it is an act of impiety for persons of our era to disparage the courageous acts of those women who gave their lives as their highest act of love.

After touring the lavish interiors of the maharaja's palace, I walked along the battlements of the once heavily fortified walls. The view looking down on the old city was excellent. The houses were built so close together that the narrow streets were hardly discernible from that height. Most of the town's two story buildings had flat roofs which served as sleeping decks in the hot summer and were also used to dry red peppers. Crumbled old city walls could be seen in the distance and beyond them were the rugged mountains and inhospitable countryside which was the beginning of the Thar desert. Perhaps a fourth of the houses were painted dark blue, which signified that the owners were *Brahmins*, members of the highest caste. The origin of the caste system, like the beginning of dowries, originally had good intent. It was founded by the great legislator Manu, who clearly perceived that humankind's natural evolution could be separated into four categories. Caste originally was not determined by one's birth, but by his or her natural tendencies. The ancient scripture the Mahabharata declares, "Neither birth nor sacraments nor study nor ancestry can decide whether a person is twice-born" (a *Brahmin* or priest); "character and conduct only can decide." In ancient India, ungenerous men of great wealth were assigned a low rank in society. It is interesting to note that throughout India's long history, a large percentage of Hindu saints have come from the non-*Brahmin* castes.

Man wearing turban. Jodhpur.

"Two generations." Men riding motor scooter. Jodhpur.

Man selling fruit. Market. Jodhpur.

Woman with child. Jaipur.

For thousands of years, the caste system traditionally provided the organizational basis of Hindu society and determined the division of the social structure to which an Indian belonged. Serious evils resulted as stratification of the caste system gradually developed through the centuries. When movement was no longer allowed between castes, exploitation began.

The four castes are: 1. those who have overcome the lower nature, are spiritually inspired, and if they are God-knowing, are able to teach and help liberate others (*Brahmins*); 2. those whose talents are administrative, executive and protective, and who try to overcome bad habits, to control the senses and to do what is right (*Kshatriyas*); 3. those ambitious for worldly gain and interested in satisfaction of the senses, who have more creative ability, such as businessmen, artists and farmers (*Vaisyas*); 4. those interested in satisfying their bodily needs and desires, who are best suited to offer service to society through physical labor (*Sudras*).

People who perform the lowest menial tasks such as cleaning toilets, sweeping streets or working in the tanning industry, which is considered ritually unclean, are outside of the caste system and are known as the "untouchables." Mahatma Gandhi did much to try to help the untouchables, and renamed them the "*Harijans*" or "children of God," although today they prefer to be called the "*Dalit*," which means "oppressed."

The Constitution of India specifically abolishes "Untouchability," and its practice in any form is forbidden and is a punishable offense under the law. It also prohibits discrimination on grounds of religion, race, caste, sex or place of birth. The Preamble to the Constitution resolves to secure justice, liberty, equality of status and opportunity for all its citizens. Historically in Hindu society, there have been legal and ritual proscriptions which prevented lower castes from participating in certain activities or imitating specified privileges reserved for the higher castes. For example, "untouchables" previously were prohibited from wearing certain types of garments or, in some villages, were not allowed to draw water from the community wells. Though the need to ameliorate their odious conditions had been recognized for a long time, it was only after Independence that an organized effort was made on a national scale.

To improve the conditions of the lower castes and certain ethnic groups, the Indian government has instituted a quota system for public jobs, parliamentary seats and university enrollment. For civil service positions, up to 60 percent of the jobs may be reserved for the disadvantaged. The southern state of Karnataka enacted a 73 percent quota for state jobs. As one might expect, such revolutionary social reforms have not been without some virulent protests from qualified persons who were not hired. Integration in the United States led to similar conflicts during its initial stages, and "affirmative action" programs are still a hotly debated topic in both countries. In spite of sweeping changes, caste continues to play an important role in contemporary India, though political power is flowing increasingly to the lower castes.

It is difficult for the Western mind to comprehend the elaborate divisions of labor into which Hindu society is divided. Each of the four castes has thousands of sub-castes, which form a hierarchy consisting of numerous small, hereditary and endogamous groups. Each sub-caste is associated with one or more types of work and, within limits, often has its own customs of dress, diet and rituals. I met a wealthy young Indian man who confided that the woman he wanted to marry would not accept him because he was not of her same sub-caste.

View from ramparts of old city. Jodhpur. Blue houses signify owners are members of Brahmin caste.

In modern India, "caste" and "class" cannot be thought of as interchangeable words. Much of the contemporary conflicts between castes have occurred in rural areas where tensions result when the lower castes through economic gain have become the upper class. Today, a *Sudra*, a member of the lowest caste, can be a government employee, a professor or an officer in the military (the *Kshatriya* caste). The problem arises when one born into the *Brahmin* caste has a *Sudra* as a superior.

All races and nations whose social customs discourage intermarriages between social classes practice certain aspects of the caste system, whether or not they understand the theory. Many profound Indian thinkers credit the caste system with having preserved the purity of the Indian people over the millenniums.

Although caste distinction still remains rigidly determined by birth, a little progress has been made in restoring the system to its original intent since independence in 1947. While time and education are very slow processes in changing humankind's thinking, they do have a wondrous way of eventually heralding change.

After the "overview" of Jodhpur from the ramparts of the fort, I decided to have a closer look. Wandering through the open markets in the old city was a photographer's dream. Women draped in colorful fabrics examined textiles, silver and handicrafts. The produce market was the most picturesque in Rajasthan. Sellers sat patiently by large baskets constructed from thick vines. Others displayed their offerings on cloth laid on the ground.

Many of those selling vegetables were elderly. Their stocks were so meager that even if they sold every item, it would not amount to much. Several underfed cows with pronounced ribs wandered contentedly among mounds of produce, reflecting the enigma of their Hindu heritage.

Woman. Jaisalmer.

Medieval walled city of Jaisalmer.

Jaisalmer

I left early the following morning by bus for the medieval walled city of Jaisalmer, located in the desert near India's western border with Pakistan.

Hundreds of years ago Jaisalmer acquired great wealth from its strategic location on the camel caravan routes between India and Central Asia. Wealthy merchants built mansions called *havelis*, which were constructed from golden-yellow sandstone, the same material used to build the rest of the city. Jaisalmer gradually lost its hegemony as ships replaced camel caravans. The devastating economic effects of World War Two and Indian partition which cut off trade routes through Pakistan resulted in Jaisalmer's becoming nearly deserted. It was revived by its military importance after the 1965 and 1971 Indo-Pakistan wars, and the increasing number of travelers who are attracted to this medieval city.

The Jaisalmer fort was built in 1156 and sits on top of a sand hill 240 feet high. About one-fourth of the old city's inhabitants live within the confines of the fort's walls, which have a total of 99 bastions around its circumference.

Walking through its narrow streets, I came upon a series of houses which had religious folk art paintings on them. I visited an exquisitely carved Jain temple that was over 500 years old. Inside around the walls were over a thousand stone figures, seated in the classical Jain pose. Round cosmology tablets and a large plaque with miniature figures were carved so intricately that the detail looked more like Japanese ivory *netsukes* (toggles) than sandstone carvings.

The major tourist attraction around Jaisalmer is a camel safari. Having once had a sunstroke in Egypt while riding a horse across the desert from the Great Pyramid of Giza to the stepped pyramid of Saqqara, I thought it would be wise not to go.

Jaisalmer, Rajasthan

I met a young English woman doctor whose husband from New Zealand was also a physician. Together with a Swiss man, we rented a Land Rover for an excursion to some of the nearby attractions. We visited a cluster of old tombs near an oasis. Their open, graceful arches allowed a full view of the barren desert sands, which seemed a fitting background for the memorials, and a reminder that none escape the eternal reaper Death. While the four of us were discussing the poverty of Rajasthan, one of India's poorest states which was experiencing the fourth year of a drought, the doctor mentioned that when living in Africa with her parents, she had seen a famine. She recounted a story of traveling with her family when they were approached for food by some starving Africans. She commented that she was glad she did not have to make the decision of whether to give them their supply of rations. The experience obviously had a profound effect on her. I believe that her rigid insistence that giving money or food would make people beggars was her way of avoiding having to deal with a situation that revived unpleasant memories. She was not unique, as I have observed many Westerners use their own mind-blocks to avoid feeling the emotional pain of others' suffering.

I was raised in a different cultural tradition from the New Zealand doctor. I, too, vividly recall an event from my childhood. Outside a movie theater in the small city of Columbus, Georgia, we approached a handicapped man sitting on the sidewalk with a metal cup filled with pencils. My grandfather, who was an immigrant from Lithuania, gave my brother and me money to give to him, with strict instructions not to accept a pencil, but at the beggar's insistence, we did. I will always remember my grandfather's scolding for our causing the man to have to buy more pencils.

Late that afternoon we arrived at the sand dunes. I took off my shoes and enjoyed walking barefoot. That was my first experience with the peace of the desert, and I could understand its eternal allure for those seeking solitude.

As I sat on top of a dune, the pure white sand was bathed in a golden glow from the setting sun, now low on the horizon. Below me was a wind-formed crater whose softly lighted sand appeared as smooth as silk.

Just behind the crater was a sand pyramid whose dark and light sides could have been a symbol for duality. Zigzag furrows created a black and white pattern on the powdery surface. Nature's show of light and shadow was spectacular.

Puppet show. Jaisalmer.

Water drawn from oasis near Jaisalmer.

Hindu pilgrimage town of Pushkar.

Pushkar

I departed Jaisalmer for the Hindu pilgrimage center of Pushkar. The bus was packed. The Rajasthani men's bright red, orange and pastel turbans gave a festive appearance to the crowded interior. I was glad when I finally arrived at my destination.

Located at the foot of a mountain on the edge of the desert, the peaceful town is built around Pushkar Lake. Having arrived after dark, I was totally unprepared for the magnificent view of this oasis which greeted me the next morning from the roof of my hotel.

Many stately white buildings and temples were built all around the lake, right up to the water's edge. Terraced stone stairs led down the gentle slope to the water, enabling bathers to approach the hallowed lake with ease. A few pilgrims were performing their morning rituals, while others were washing their clothes. The blurred images of the white edifices were reflected in the calm, azure water. The tranquil lake gave the town an appearance of a bygone era unspoiled by mechanization.

Climbing to several small temples on the steep mountains offered a test of stamina to the pilgrims' devotion. The few green trees were in stark contrast to the yellow sands of the desert, which stretched as far as I could see.

That night at dinner I had a delicious vegetable dish served with *kachori*, freshly baked bread filled with onions. The gourmet meal cost less than a dollar. On the way back to my hotel, I got rid of the *prashad* (sweets) in my pocket, which I had received at a temple earlier in the day. A hungry cow in the narrow street accepted the offering, which had been rejected by two dogs whose haunt near a sweet stall had taught them to be more discriminating.

Sweets with edible thin silver coverings. Pushkar.

Man cooking sweets. Pushkar.

Since it was a pilgrimage center, Pushkar had many shops which sold delicious sweets. Small pieces of candy wrapped in thin sheets of pure silver were neatly stacked on counters in arrangements up to a foot high. The silver wrapping was eaten with the sweet, for in India, ingesting silver is thought to be good for one's health.

Men were cooking desserts in skillets over an open fire. Bowls containing milk, sugar and other ingredients were sitting uncovered to cool, while flies congregated on the rims to sample the savory sweets. A few of the braver and greedier two-winged insects, not satisfied with a fly's portion, ventured into the center where they gorged themselves to death, becoming trapped as the contents thickened.

Early the next morning I boarded a crowded bus which took me over the craggy mountain separating Pushkar from nearby Ajmer. I had enjoyed my visit and felt refreshed from my rest.

Ajmer is an interesting city which has a long Muslim history. It is built around a large lake and located at the base of barren hills. Today it is a major pilgrimage site during Ramadan.

One of India's most sacred sites for Muslims is the *Dargah* (a tomb of a holy man). The complex is in honor of a Sufi saint who came to Ajmer in 1192. Located outside the entrance gate, proprietors sat proudly at their flower stalls. They had so neatly arranged brightly colored blossoms in bins that from a distance I thought that they were sweets.

Red peppers. Market. Ajmer.

Flower stall. Tomb (Dargah) of a Sufi (Muslim) saint. Ajmer.

Entrance, Adhai-din-ka-jhonpra Mosque. Ajmer.

Carved marble interior of Vimala Sha Temple. Jain. Mt. Abu, 1032 A.D.

Mt. Abu

My travels next took me to Mt. Abu. The rugged mountains in that part of Rajasthan reminded me of Wales. At a rest stop in a small town during my long bus trip, many passengers bought something to drink. It was buffalo milk that was being boiled over an open fire. The vendor skimmed a little cream from the surface of the steaming liquid and placed it in each glass. The hot drink of milk, sugar and curd tasted delicious.

Located at an elevation of over 3,600 feet, Mt. Abu is the only "hill station" in the state of Rajasthan. The small town has a population of 13,000 and is built on a plateau.

Besides serving as a mountain retreat during the scorching Indian summers, Mt. Abu is an important pilgrimage point for members of the Jain religion because of the intricately carved Dilwara Temples. The town also is a favorite spot for couples on their honeymoon. Since it was winter, the hill town was not crowded.

I took a bus tour to the famous Jain Dilwara Temples. The temples are among the finest examples of Jain architecture in India and were built during the late Medieval period from 1032 to 1233. The delicacy of the interior of the earlier and more important Vimala Sha Temple takes marble carving to unsurpassed heights. The columns were connected by filigreed buttresses that reach to the ceiling. The inverted "V"-shaped architectural supports probably shifted to the columns some of the heavy weight from the marble domed ceiling, similar to the vaulting of a Roman aqueduct.

Surrounding the main temple is a courtyard that was made distinctive by 58 small cells once used by Jain ascetics. White marble porticoes marked the entrance to each small enclosure, which contain various marble statues of Jain saints.

The end of the plateau is the highest point in the state of Rajasthan (5,170 feet) which has a nice view of the plains below. As we neared the scenic overlook, I observed several orthodox Jain men dressed in white, wearing gauze masks over their faces. They were sweeping the path in front of them to avoid inadvertently stepping on insects.

After the half day tour was completed, I climbed into the back of a crowded jeep that functioned as a mini-bus. Its fixed route from downtown to the Jain temple provided me with a quick and inexpensive ride to the *ashram* where I was staying. When I returned, the *sadhu* had prepared a delicious lunch for me consisting of *dahl* (lentils), potatoes, a vegetable dish I could not identify, rice and *chapatis*. He gave me such huge servings that I could not eat it all.

Later that afternoon while we were sitting outside in the sunshine, two cows walking by responded immediately when he called to them, and enjoyed being fed my uneaten *chapatis*. His good nature was evident while feeding them, even as he pretended to be firm when he sent them away. He returned to his chair with a chuckle and a gleam in his eyes.

With the agility of a young man, the old *sadhu* walked on the narrow rounded top of the *ashram* wall while he plucked flowers to grace the altars. On a tour of the grounds earlier that morning, he nimbly led me down a steep, rocky ledge.

I noticed that the skin on his feet was splitting, presumably from exposure to the cold temperature, which that morning covered the ground with frost. He wore a sweater and wool hat, but his lower body was covered only by a thin, cotton *lungi* (sarong). He washed the temple daily and when he returned from his duties, I could tell his hands and feet were freezing from the way he warmed them around his small fire. I enjoyed being in his loving, peaceful presence, and always will remember fondly my two days with the "gentle giant."

I left Mt. Abu by bus to go to Ahmedabad, located in the neighboring state of Gujarat. Seated on one side of me was an Indian couple who were on their honeymoon. They were wearing blue jeans which is considered chic for newlyweds to wear in rustic areas. The road was very bumpy, and since we were sitting over the rear wheels of the bus, we were bounced off our seats frequently. She took advantage of each occasion to utter a cute, soft "shriek," much like a teenager, which always got her a hug or loving touch from her husband. Most Hindus do not display affection publicly, and except for children, that was the first time I had seen it done.

Dancing apsaras (heavenly nymphs) on marble pillar. Dilwara Temple. Jain. Mt. Abu, ca. 13th century.

Sculptural detail, Vimala Sha Temple. Jain. Mt. Abu, 1032 A.D.

Dwarkanath Temple at sunset, Dwarka, Gujarat

Chapter Five

The West

◁ *Opposite*
Standing Buddha.
Ajanta, Cave 19.
Gupta Dynasty, late
5th century.

The West: Gujarat and Maharashtra

Few tourists spend much time in the state of Gujarat, which is located between Bombay and Rajasthan. Yet, I would consider the Jain mountaintop pilgrimage center of Palitana to be an exceptional place which should not be missed. It has over 850 temples, some almost 1,000 years old. It is a five hour bus trip from Ahmedabad, where Mahatma Gandhi established Sabarmati Ashram, his headquarters during the long struggle for Indian independence against the British. I enjoyed my visit to Dwarka, a picturesque seaside pilgrimage town where Lord Krishna once had his kingdom.

The isolated westernmost part of Gujarat known as the Kutch has retained much of its tradition and I was glad that I made the journey to the old walled city of Bhuj. Inside the Swaminarayan Temple, with its richly decorated shrines, I met an Indian resident whose daughter now lives in my hometown of Columbus, Georgia. Karma!

Bombay, the capital of Maharashtra, serves as an international gateway to India. Located a full day's journey northeast of the modern city are the world-famous Ajanta and Ellora caves. I found Ajanta to be the most interesting place which I visited in all of India.

Priests tossing rice into sacred fire (yajna), symbolizing burning one's bad karma as the mind becomes purified. Nuns are wearing red saris and shawls. Swaminarayan Temple. Bhuj, Gujarat.

Shrine figures, Swaminarayan Temple. Bhuj, Gujarat.

Moon behind Dwarkanath Temple at sunrise. Dwarka, Gujarat. Dwarkanath is a title of Lord Krishna.

"He who perceives Me everywhere and beholds everything in Me, never loses sight of Me, nor do I ever lose sight of him."
    Bhagavan Krishna
    Bhagavad Gita VI:30.

Painting of Lord Krishna, as charioteer counseling Prince Arjuna at the historic battle of Kurukshetra.

Gujarat

Ahmedabad

Ahmedabad is one of India's major industrial cities with over three million people. It is better known for its textile industry, but it has some of the finest examples of Islamic architecture in India.

Though the city is noisy and polluted, I liked it. The streets were narrow and crowded with all kinds of vehicles and pedestrians. It seemed to me that the street's center line served as nothing more than a median, delineating equal distance on either side. Drivers had little respect for its presence. The rules for driving in India are mainly "might makes right." Trucks forced cars off the road, cars forced three wheel motor rickshaws and motor scooters off the road and pedestrians had to fend for themselves.

Although I have driven automobiles in many parts of the world, I would never attempt to drive in most Indian cities. There are few traffic lights and even major intersections do not have policemen to direct traffic. The lack of traffic patterns leads to chaotic conditions; therefore, it is important to be definite in one's intention so the other driver knows which way to maneuver to avoid an accident. There were so many "near misses" that even though I became accustomed to them, I still had many moments of consternation and frequently asked my drivers to slow down.

Ahmedabad can be very hot in the summer. The Mughal Emperor Jehangir, who evidently was not overly fond of the city, called it Gardabad, "the City of Dust." On one of my visits, the temperature reached 119 degrees Fahrenheit. It was the hottest weather I had ever encountered.

The Monsoon

The hot Indian summer starts near the end of March, and by June every one has "had it" with the heat. Suddenly the sky becomes gray, and big drops of long awaited rain begin to fall. There is a refreshing smell as water hits the parched earth. One has to be there to appreciate it.

Eventually the rain comes down in torrents so thick that you cannot even see your hand. People flock to the streets — adults wearing clothes and children not. To Indians, the rain is bliss — heaven sent. Many men take their shirts off and enjoy the sensation of the rain striking their bare skin.

Getting drenched together with a loved one is considered very romantic. A candlelight dinner would never do for Indians what getting wet in the monsoon does. It is joyful rejuvenation of both man and earth. If the monsoon is delayed or shortened, it causes anxiety and disaster. The land must get one year's worth of rain in four to five weeks. When the thunderstorms start, it can be 110 degrees, but the temperature abruptly drops to the 70s. Then the sun comes out for a few days before the storms begin again. The pattern repeats for the duration of the monsoon. Next comes a visual feast. Everything becomes green. Flowers bloom everywhere. Gradually the intensity and frequency of the rain diminishes and then it stops. It is over for another year.

Modhera

About 70 miles northwest of Ahmedabad is the Sun Temple of Modhera. I was eager to visit the temple because of a strange occurrence which happened to me while I was in Goa. When eating breakfast near the beach one morning in an almost empty restaurant, an Indian man approached my table. Placing a magazine in front of me that was opened to color photographs of a temple located about a thousand miles away in Gujarat, he said to me: "You should go there." My body immediately tingled as if in confirmation of his directive. Writing down the name and location of the temple, I put the encounter out of my mind.

Modhera is the temple that was pictured in the magazine which was thrust upon me in Goa. My host Rakesh and the family's young house boy were happy to accompany me on the journey. Upon entering the sacred shrine room, once dedicated to the Sun God Surya, I felt peaceful vibrations, somehow connected to the ruined temple's past. It was as if the peaceful currents flowed directly into my physical body. To be sure I was not imagining it, I would go outside for comparison and then return to the sacred precinct. Of the hundreds of temples I visited in India, that was the site where I was most aware of the spiritual vibrations. Why the man in Goa approached me with the magazine article on Modhera remains one of the enigmas of my life.

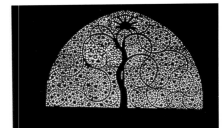

Carved stone window with Tree of Life motif. Sidi Saiyad's Mosque. Ahmedabad, Gujarat.

Muslim reading Koran, early morning. Jami Mosque, Ahmedabad. Built in 1424.

Jain temples on top of holy mountain at Palitana. Gujarat.

Palitana

After returning to Ahmedabad, I saw a picture in a downtown office building which caught my fancy. When I inquired about it, I was told that those were the Jain temples in southwest Gujarat on top of the holy mountain at Palitana. I knew that I would go there, and early the following morning I went to the bus station.

Indian bus stations often are chaotic. Sometimes buses leave from designated platforms, and other times they just stop in a general area, where people push and shove to get aboard. If the bus does not leave from a designated bay, it can be very confusing for a foreigner. In all of my travels throughout India, someone always came forward whenever I needed help. In this instance, it was a young boy selling newspapers who showed me my bus when it arrived. The trip to Palitana took almost five hours.

Once an important religious movement in India, the Jains now comprise less than one percent of India's population. The religion is contemporaneous with Buddhism, and has some similarities. It was founded in the sixth century B.C. by Mahavira (Great Spirit), the twenty-fourth and last of the Jain saints called *Tirthankaras*. The *Tirthankaras*, "the ones who lead to the other shore," are also called *jinas* (victors or heroes), and their followers are called Jains, the sons of victors.

Jains conceive the universe to be infinite, and believe that it was not created by a deity; that the cosmos consists of imperishable particles, some too small to be seen, and all of which have souls.

The Jain belief in *ahimsa*, reverence for all life and the avoidance of injury to all living things, accounts for orthodox Jains wearing gauze masks over the face to prevent accidentally swallowing an insect. They also carry small brooms to sweep tiny insects from their paths as they walk. This belief leads to the observance of strict vegetarianism.

Jainism, like Buddhism, had spread throughout most of India, and by the 16th century it had established a solid following in the mercantile districts of western India. Persecution forced the Jains to leave southern India, but the religion flourished in the west, where wealthy merchants gained merit by building temples and monasteries. Numerous Jain edifices, which either survived the destructive Muslim invasions or were restored or commissioned afterwards, remain today in Gujarat and western Rajasthan.

The top of the mountain at Palitana is known as Shatrunjaya, the "Place of Victory," and is one of the holiest Jain pilgrimage sites. Over a period of 900 years, 863 temples have been constructed atop this peak. The earliest temples were built during the 11th century, but they were destroyed in the 14th and 15th centuries by the Muslims, who with few exceptions were not known for their religious tolerance. The existing temples date from the 1500s to the present.

I engaged a horse cart in front of my hotel to take me to the base of the famous mountain, which was a little over a mile away. Because of Jain respect for all life no leather, including shoes and watch bands, may be worn on the sacred mountain. As I ascended the hundreds of steps to the summit, I appreciated the Herculean effort that must have gone into transporting the building materials for the temples. Those whose age or health did not permit physical exertion could hire a *dooli* (swing chair), which was supported from the shoulders of two porters. The cost of being carried up the steep incline was determined partially by the weight of the rider.

As I neared the summit, I saw high walls which gave the hilltop the appearance of a fortress. Inside the sacred precinct, temples were grouped into nine separate compounds or *tunks*, each with a central temple, surrounded by many minor ones. The narrow streets reminded me of the medieval walled cities of Europe. From the top of the walls, there was a panoramic view of the Gulf of Cambay. The sparkling azure water provided a contrast to the parched, rugged countryside.

The most famous temple is dedicated to the first Jain *Tirthankara*, Shri Adinatha. Like the Jain temples at Mt. Abu, these were among the most intricately carved interiors I had ever seen. The filigree carvings gave credence to the traditional story that the sculptors did not carve the marble with tools, but worked it with abrasive cords, and were paid at the end of each day according to the size of the pile of marble dust they had accumulated!

Overhead, elaborate massive decorations on the ceiling transformed marble into intricate geometric designs of lace, which hung downward like stalactic snowflakes, clustered together to form a canopy.

As sunset approached, I headed toward the main gate because no one was allowed to remain on the mountain after dusk. Early the following morning, I departed for Ahmedabad.

Jain woman being carried up mountain in swing chair. Palitana, Gujarat.

Carved marble ceiling, Jain temple. Palitana, Gujarat.

"Step well" (well with steps leading down to it), one of the largest and finest examples of its kind. Patan, Gujarat. Built ca. 1050 A.D.

Detail of sculptures near bottom of step well. Patan, Gujarat.

Ajanta and Ellora Caves

The train arrived early the next morning in Jalgaon, where I boarded a local bus to Ajanta. Admittance to the caves was free that day but did not include an inexpensive "light ticket." Without a light ticket, the caretaker would not shine his dim light on the famous frescoes, leaving the viewer in almost total darkness. A few of the more important caves had adequate lighting.

Many school children were visiting the caves that day. They were friendly and inquisitive and every few minutes one of them asked me, "What country are you from?" Because of the infrequency of American tourists to Ajanta, most did not guess that I was from the United States. Indians enjoy having their pictures taken by and with foreigners and consider it prestigious.

Several Indian tourists whom I met gave me their addresses, and extended invitations for me to visit them. School children sang an Indian song for me, and a young girl did a "disco" dance. With the least encouragement, they would grin and speak to me in English. The sharing of friendship with both the children and adults was almost as memorable to me as the famous caves.

The 29 caves at Ajanta are carved into a steep, horseshoe-shaped gorge which was formed by a small river flowing at its base. The Buddhist caves at Ajanta predate those of Ellora and contain some of the oldest surviving examples of Indian paintings. The caves were carved during a 700 year period from the second century B.C. to the seventh century A.D., when Buddhism was waning in India. Once abandoned, the rock-cut sanctuaries became overgrown and lost. They were not discovered until 1817, when a British hunting party in quest of tigers stumbled upon them, and their splendor again was known to the world.

A wide walkway along the ravine's wall makes the caves easily accessible. Many of them have large columns, with intricately carved capitals, giving the illusion that they are supporting the massive sanctuaries. The columns actually were not needed architecturally, since all of the caves were hollowed out from rock.

The caves originally served as monasteries (*viharas*), but by the fifth century A.D., their purpose was extended to include shrines for worship (*chaityas*). I was more inspired by the earlier Hinayana Buddhist caves than I was by the later and more elaborate Mahayana ones. Most of the realistic paintings portrayed the various incarnations of the Buddha, and were depicted in contemporary settings of the artists' world. A variety of muted colors gave the frescoes a venerable look.

Elaborately carved porches covered with images of the Buddha were attached to the outer facade of some caves. They made impressive entrances to the sanctuaries which were adorned with graceful columns and frescoes. The ceiling of a few of them emulated in stone the vaulted arches of timber, much like an early Gothic cathedral. A large image of the Buddha peered out from a darkened shrine room. The superb sculptures at Ajanta and Ellora compare favorably to religious carvings of the Greco-Roman period.

Buddhist caves at Ajanta. Maharashtra.

*Wall painting of the Bodhisattva Padmapani holding a lotus. Ajanta Cave 1.
Gupta Dynasty, late 5th century A.D.*

*Large seated
Buddha and
other statuary.
Ajanta
Caves.*

Wall painting of Princess Arundati in a swing. Ajanta Cave 2. Gupta Dynasty, 5th - 6th century A.D.

Buddhas carved in bold relief. Ajanta Caves.

Veranda of Cave 2 at Ajanta.
5th - 6th century A.D.

Near Aurangabad are the caves at Ellora. The 29 caves at Ajanta are all Buddhist. At Ellora, 12 caves are Buddhist, 17 are Hindu and 5 are Jain. It is thought that the builders of Ajanta moved to Ellora when construction at the earlier site abruptly halted, circa seventh century A.D.

The Ellora caves, which were an old pilgrimage center for Buddhists, Hindus and Jains, are carved into an escarpment of volcanic stone, which rises above the plain of the Northern Deccan plateau. While Ajanta is better known for its paintings, Ellora is one of the greatest of all Indian sites for sculpture. The masterpiece and central attraction at Ellora is Kailasanatha Temple which rises almost 100 feet above the carved courtyard floor. Like the other elaborate cave-temples at Ajanta, meticulous advanced planning of the entire project was essential, because unlike conventional architecture, success depended on what was removed rather than what was constructed. The huge temple covers twice the area of the Parthenon in Athens and is almost twice as high.

"Preaching" Buddha carved on a stupa. Ellora, Cave 10. Ca. 700 - 750 A.D.

Bombay

Bombay is India's largest and most industrialized city with over 13 million inhabitants. It was ceded to Portugal in the 16th century, before the British government took control. By the early 18th century, it had become the British East India Company's headquarters for trade on the west coast of India.

Bombay has retained its title of "The Gateway to India." Not surprisingly, it is India's most cosmopolitan city, with a modern stock exchange in which 65 percent of middle-class and upper middle-class families buy shares.

Overlooking the city from the top of Malabar Hill are the formal "Hanging Gardens." Located next to the gardens, but carefully concealed from view, are the Parsi "Towers of Silence." The Parsis are followers of Zoroastrianism, one of the oldest religions in the world. The religion was founded in Persia by the prophet Zarathustra (Zoroaster). Because Parsis believe in the purity of the elements (earth, water, fire, air) and do not wish to pollute them, they do not cremate or bury their dead. Instead, the corpses are placed within the "Towers of Silence" where vultures do the rest.

Seeking to escape persecution in Persia, the Parsis fled to Bombay in 1670, and built their first "Tower of Silence" five years later. Though only about 85,000 Parsis currently live in India, because of their philanthropy and success in commerce and industry, their influence far exceeds their numbers.

During my visit to Bombay, I stayed in the suburb of Vile Parle West with an Indian family. One day after lunch, Parul, who was about 18 years old, asked me if I would accompany her and three friends to visit Mahalaxmi Temple in downtown Bombay. I was delighted to go, of course.

Mahalaxmi Temple, Bombay's oldest temple, sits majestically on a hill overlooking the Arabian Sea. It is dedicated to Lakshmi, the goddess of wealth, an appropriate patron deity for this thriving city of commerce.

Before entering Hindu temples and homes, a person removes his shoes. Unlike Western churches and synagogues, there are no pews inside on which to sit. The interior is open space, except for the altar at the rear of the temple. Lengthy services and sermons have no function here. Prayer books are not necessary to offer the untutored chords of one's heart. Spontaneity of devotion requires no formal structuring.

With a basket of flowers and sweets as an offering from all of us, we made our way forward, passing through a constant stream of pilgrims coming from the altar. A tall, impressive image of Lakshmi was almost completely covered in garlands of flowers.

Gateway of India, Taj Mahal Hotel and Taj Intercontinental. Bombay, Maharashtra.

Two Hindu priests were sitting on the altar in front of the statue of Lakshmi. I stood in front of one of the seated priests, not knowing what to do. One of our group, who was standing behind me, observed my predicament and pushed my arms forward toward the priests. One of them took the basket from me. Then placing the fingers and palms of both hands together we *pranamed* to the Goddess Lakshmi in a ritual gesture of respect.

The ritual conducted by the priests was clever. While intoning a prayer, he placed the offering at Lakshmi's feet. Then he picked up an offering that had already been accepted and blessed by the goddess and distributed it to the pilgrims. The eagerly sought sweets known as *prashad* are believed to be divinely blessed. Those who remain at the altar receive an ochre mark on their "spiritual eye."

Staying in an Indian home enabled me to learn about the local customs. To my surprise, what is correct etiquette in America is not in India. Whenever I thanked anyone for something, I was told that I must not do that. After asking many questions, I concluded that "thank you" is only used in formal situations. Among close friends and family no words of thanks are necessary, since the other person already knows how much he or she is appreciated.

The amount of affection that Seema and her two sisters gave to her eleven month old son, Karan, touched my heart. Nandini, the middle sister, referred to herself as his second mother, and indeed she was. When I spoke to Seema about how much time she spent playing with her son, she replied that, "We in India do not have much materially to give our children, so we make up for it by giving a lot of love." My personal feelings about the importance of parental love were echoed by Mother Teresa when she said to an American couple, "I have seen the starving (on the streets of Calcutta), but in your country I have seen an even greater hunger. That is the hunger to be loved. No place in all of my travels have I seen such loneliness as I have seen in the poverty of affluence in America."

That evening a friend stopped by after dinner. He explained to me a young man's duty to his family. In the West, after graduating from high school or college, children often move away from home, pursuing their own interests, making a filial as well as a physical break. Because of traditional values which hold the family as a nuclear unit, this would be unthinkable in India. The children are expected not only to work for the family and to take care of their parents in their old age, but also to put family needs before personal needs. An unmarried man is even expected to provide for his nieces and nephews before himself.

Girl sitting on shore of Arabian Sea behind Mahalaxmi Temple. Bombay.

Children's ride, Juhu Beach. Bombay.

While walking in the neighborhood one day, I passed a two story building with a low fence around it where a large group of well-dressed women were eagerly waiting. The event looked promising, so I decided to wait and see what developed. In a short time, the doors opened and young schoolboys came running out. They were dressed in uniforms of tan shirts and shorts like boy scouts. A few moments later the girls came out, which led me to believe that boys and girls are taught in separate classes, according to the custom of ancient Hindu tradition. The mothers called and waved to their children and affectionately hugged and greeted them. It was hard for me to believe that the children received such a warm welcome every day after school. In the West one does not see this display of emotion on a daily basis and it was quite a contrast to Western "car pools." It was the type of greeting I might have expected after returning home from a two month summer camp.

Surat, Gujarat

From Bombay, I took a train to Surat, located about 150 miles north in the state of Gujarat. I was going there to visit a couple, both medical doctors, whom I had met the previous year in California at a yoga convocation. They were expecting me, and Ajay picked me up at the station in his car. I was happy to be traveling first class again!

After a delicious lunch, they acquainted me with various aspects of Indian life. Jayshree explained that the child is next in importance to God, and until the child is four to five years old, the parents make sacrifices and stay at home as much as possible. It is incomprehensible to a Hindu how American mothers leave their children so frequently.

While Ajay was visiting the United States, there had been a plane crash, and only one child survived. Ajay was amazed at the statement of the grandparent, who had not yet decided the "fate" of the boy. A Hindu grandparent, regardless of his circumstances, would have adopted that child and raised him as his own.

The following day, one of Ajay's best friends had lunch with us. I liked him immediately. Dr. Patel explained to me that there is no formality in Indian friendships, and that the expression of "thank you" is a phrase which leads to insincerity and perfunctory habit. He said that it is okay to express an occasional thank you, but it is the warmth of the eyes and heart that reveal true feelings, making speech unnecessary. He added, "Words are meaningless without actions. We don't say 'I love you,' we just show it."

Homes in the state of Gujarat have a distinctive feature that sets them apart from the rest of India. Most of them have large swings inside. Ajay's swing was supported by a metal frame, while Dr. Patel's was connected to the ceiling by two chains. Because one of my earliest and happiest memories from childhood is swinging with my parents and older brother in a glider on our front porch, I never miss an opportunity to sit on a swing. When my preference became known, my hosts would get up if sitting to make room for me. Dr. Patel often would sit next to me on his swing, and we both enjoyed seeing how high we could go in his parlor.

A few days later, Dr. Patel invited me to accompany him on a trip to visit his parents, who lived in a small village several hundred miles north. We arrived at his parents' home in time for dinner. Since the "guest is God," it always was a culinary delight for me to dine in an Indian home. I was served food until I had to adamantly refuse it being placed on my plate.

Later that evening, Dr. Patel took me to the home of his good friend, who was the local Sanskrit teacher. There were no lights on when we arrived, but after knocking, someone opened the door and led us up to a darkened loft. A small light was turned on for us, and we quickly took a seat among the many children who had come to see the weekly television episode of the religious epic, the Mahabharata.

When the program was over, they left without speaking a word. I wondered if they were consciously practicing silence, a precursor of peace. They had been watching one of the few television sets in the village. It seemed that the entire nation came to a halt every Friday evening from 9:00 to 10:00 p.m., when people watched the exciting dramatization of an ancient scripture. I, too, had seen the series during my previous two weeks in Bombay and Surat. I learned later that this program was watched by more people than any other ever shown on Indian television. This is not surprising, considering the spiritual nature of the Hindu people.

The next morning I met Dr. Patel's cousin from Canada. Both he and his sister had returned to India to get married. He explained that he had met many Canadian girls whom he liked, but did not trust marrying them, and added, "If you know what I mean!" He and his sister had placed ads in the newspaper of a nearby city which drew many responses. He interviewed over sixty girls before making his selection.

Marriage

In most Indian families, marriages are still arranged, although today the children usually have a say in the selection process. The custom of not seeing one's spouse until the arrival at the marriage ceremony is a thing of the past. The potential marriage partners get to meet in the presence of their parents, to see if they satisfy each other's physical requirements and to talk with one another to determine if they are compatible. If both families agree after that first stage, then their horoscopes are exchanged and given to astrologers to ascertain if they are well-matched.

One family I stayed with was concerned because their son had rejected the first 24 girls they had arranged for him to meet! In Bombay, when I asked Nandini, who was a liberated medical student, if her father would play a role in the selection process of her husband, she seemed indignant and replied that she would not think of marrying someone of whom her father did not approve, although one of her older sisters had.

The West

Westerners who are unfamiliar with Hindu culture cannot understand how arranged marriages are more successful than the Western process of choosing one's own mate. But they are. Hindu marriages are based on the principles of establishing friendship first, which forms a basis for a permanent relationship, and then developing love for each other. Currently in the West, nearly one out of every two marriages ends in divorce. Could it be because the selection of one's mate usually is based on short-term emotional considerations and sex appeal, with neither party seeking the advice of his or her parents or minister?

The Hindu scripture, the <u>Ramayana,</u> teaches children from an early age the correct behavior for an ideal marriage. In this epic, Rama and Sita, husband and wife, have the perfect marriage. Rama would never look at another woman, and Sita would never look at another man. In one chapter, an older woman tells Sita the attributes that an ideal wife should cultivate. It is interesting to note that Rama and Sita have attained a perfect relationship because they both have overcome the temptations of the senses. Divorces, until recently, were rare in Hindu marriages, and there is a saying that "To separate the marriage is to displease God." Nandini explained to me that no matter what happens, "We always think of giving marriage a chance."

A doctor I met on a train commented that "Hindu husbands and wives have arguments, but there are limits beyond which we do not go." Another Hindu traveler I met on a different trip explained that "Indian women do not go to health spas to keep their figures trim like Western women, and after having babies, they often get plump. Yet we would never think of looking elsewhere." I now had the answer to my oft pondered question of what had Hindu men done to deserve, possibly, the most loyal, devoted wives in the world. The answer: the Hindu husband's love — although often not shown outwardly — is reflected in his purity. Traditional Hindu values are breaking down rapidly, however, in the onslaught of Indian desire for Western technology and materialism.

Hindu women have an inner power and serenity that is seldom seen in the battle of the sexes in the West. At several social gatherings when men were flaunting their egos, as males tend to do in the presence of women, I observed one wife wink at another wife, unseen by their husbands. Men may think that they run India but its greatness actually is her women. They are the devotional ones who hold the marriage, family and heterogeneous country together.

A brief story will illustrate the above point. On my return trip to America, I began a conversation with an Indian flight attendant. The young Hindu lady, who was living in Hong Kong, appeared "liberated" in a Western sense. When I asked her if she would be willing to subordinate her career and ego for a higher cause of marriage, without hesitation she replied, "Of course. What do you think makes us such good wives?"

I learned in a most unexpected way the life-long commitment a Hindu woman takes into a relationship. When visiting Indian friends in Central India, a 15 year old girl asked if I could get her a pen pal in America. When I was preparing to leave a week later, she had not returned, so I sent for her. As she handed me her address, she confided that the reason she had not come back was because she was not sure that she could commit to writing to someone for the rest of her life!

Groom's flower covered automobile. Bombay.

Groom and his sister arriving for wedding. Gujarat.

Wedding guests, reluctant to be photographed. Gujarat.

Perhaps one reason marriages are so unsuccessful in the West today is that most occidentals do not even understand the principles on which to base a spiritual marriage. The famous yogi and world teacher Paramahansa Yogananda, author of <u>Autobiography of a Yogi</u>, which is one of the ten all time best selling autobiographies, has some cogent comments on the spiritual purposes of marriage. Yogananda explains that in man, reason is predominant, and in woman, feeling is the uppermost characteristic. Through marriage, man brings out the hidden reason in woman, and woman brings out the hidden feeling in man. All men can appreciate the saying which testifies to woman's emotional nature: "Woman convinced against her will, is of the same opinion still!" Man is just as one-sided, and acts too much from the intellect and not enough from his heart, as all women know. Through a spiritual marriage, each helps to balance the other's temperament.

By displaying love, friendship, loyalty, respect and other noble qualities for each other, the two souls merge into perfect harmony. But perfect harmony is not the goal of marriage, just as it is not the goal for one wave blown by the wind of delusion to merge with another wave. The goal is for both waves to dissolve back into the sea. Once husband and wife become one with each other, their united hearts are offered to God and merged back into the "ocean of Spirit." Spiritual marriage, when properly understood, becomes a beautiful (but often difficult!) path to God.

The following story was told to me by a close friend of the family mentioned. While a woman was cooking a meal on a gas burner, her clothes caught fire. She did not scream for help until she was engulfed in flames. When her husband entered the kitchen, he realized he could not save her. His only thought was to comfort her in her final moments so he embraced her. She died almost immediately and he died a few hours later.

When traveling by train one day, I met an Indian who asked me if I thought I would ever marry. I answered, "Yes, if I ever met someone with whom I had soul unity." Looking at me with a smile he replied, "Soul unity comes through many years of marriage."

Marriage is not a prerequisite for attaining balance between feeling and reason if an individual experiences a human relationship of pure love or friendship. But unconditional love must be perfected first on the physical plane, before divine love can be achieved on the spiritual plane. If one cannot conquer human hearts, one will never win the heart of God.

Dowries

Dr. Patel informed me one morning that we were going to visit his mother's family who lived in a nearby village. Upon entering their house, we were offered the customary glass of water, but I was afraid to drink it in fear of contracting amoebic dysentery. Unlike previous situations when I refused, this time my conscience silently broadcast a loud and clear message that I should accept the water. Before drinking it, I prayed to God from the depth of my soul: "Lord, you know that I am drinking this water against my better judgment, in order not to hurt these people's feelings, so please protect me!" Instantly, a strange sensation came over me and I knew my prayer had been answered. From that moment onward, I drank tap water, water from the holy Ganges River and water from various sources with no adverse consequences. I truly believe that because of my deep love for Indians, and my desire to have them know that their simple hospitality was sufficient for an American, I received a special dispensation from God. Later in America when I met an Indian medical doctor, he was amazed to learn that I drank the water and ate any food I wanted. He said that even he could not do that without getting sick, and explained how my faith had increased my stomach's secretion of hydrochloric acid, which killed germs and had prevented me from becoming ill!

After I drank the glass of water offered me, I felt good for having followed my conscience. Later, we were invited to sit down on the floor for lunch, but Dr. Patel's mother's family did not eat with us as I had expected them to. They were our servers! After we finished our multiple course dinner, they sat down and ate their meal. When we were preparing to leave, her mother's family offered money to Dr. Patel's father, which is the custom when the husband visits his wife's family. He did not want to accept it, but finally, he took some minuscule amount to satisfy them.

While dowries are much abused by the groom's family in India, one should remember that the principle is to insure that the girl gets a fair portion of her father's wealth. Most of the educated women in India today refuse to marry a man if he or his family demands a dowry. That was certainly the case of all of the daughters of families whom I knew. There are also numerous societies which oppose dowries and promote its abolition. It is primarily in rural areas and among less educated sub-castes where the custom still prevails. Like most abuses in India's ancient traditions, things are changing for the better.

Though the Dowry Prohibition Act of 1961 clearly abolishes dowries, often the bride's family agrees to pay one. The oppressive dowry does not end with matrimonial contracts. For example, the family of the bride is expected to continually provide nice gifts to the groom on special occasions, or when the groom comes to visit. Dowries can even ruin a family financially, depending on the ambitions that the bride's family has for their daughter. Sensational newspapers are filled with accounts of cruelties, beatings and even murders of women by husbands who thought their dowries were insufficient. A lawyer I spoke to informed me that it is difficult to prove that a dowry was demanded, but when conclusive evidence is available, a jail sentence usually is served. Exceptions are made for the State of Jammu and Kashmir and does not include certain Muslim marriage practices which are regulated by their own religious laws.

The dowry system is the chief cause for families not wanting to have daughters. With medical technology now able to determine the sex of a fetus (amniocentesis), an alarming percentage of female fetuses were being aborted, especially in the villages where the dowry tradition is still binding. To end that practice, a law was passed which prohibits Indian doctors telling parents in advance the sex of their baby.

Not all of India is patriarchal. In some regions of the state of Kerala in South India, the families are matriarchal. Women are the decision makers and play a dominant role. I was told that all over India, the maternal uncle often plays a key role in Hindu families.

In all of the families I visited, women seemed to have the same status that they do in the West. Without exception, the husbands helped clear the dishes from the table after the meals, and they often performed other kitchen chores.

I enjoyed my visit with Dr. Patel's family. My last day spent there was particularly memorable because Dr. Patel took me to a nearby village to meet a yogi (a practitioner of yoga). He lived in a small whitewashed house with a faded religious painting on the front. For 14 years he had not left his small compound, which he had made into a temple. He depended entirely on contributions and food which villagers left for him. Since he spoke no English, Dr. Patel served as an interpreter.

I was concerned when the yogi said that I had made a mistake in coming to India. Upon further questioning, he said that I could not find what I was looking for there. Like a swami we had met a few days previously, he was telling me that God was inside. He would not answer my questions directly, and often responded that God manifests through everything, and that I should see God in all and serve God in all.

The yogi said that we should always act from our heart, as devotion is necessary to open that center of feeling. He stated that marriage was the greatest delusion (if it is not based on spiritual principles), and ties us to the physical world, separating us from God. He commented that it was good that I had never married, and that I should just serve God.

He was very particular about performing his spiritual duties at specific times, possibly to establish regular habits. In response to a question about healing the body, he said that a lady who had recently come to him with an incurable medical disease had gotten well after he gave her something to take.[1] He mentioned that someone else who visited him had a similar experience. Thanking him for his advice and leaving a donation inside his shrine, we knelt and respectfully touched his feet and departed with his blessings.

Yogi. Gujarat. Painting depicts prelude to creation with Vishnu reclining on the cosmic serpent Ananta on the waters of Nara.

Schoolgirls, Church of the Immaculate Conception, Panjim, Goa.

Chapter Six

The South

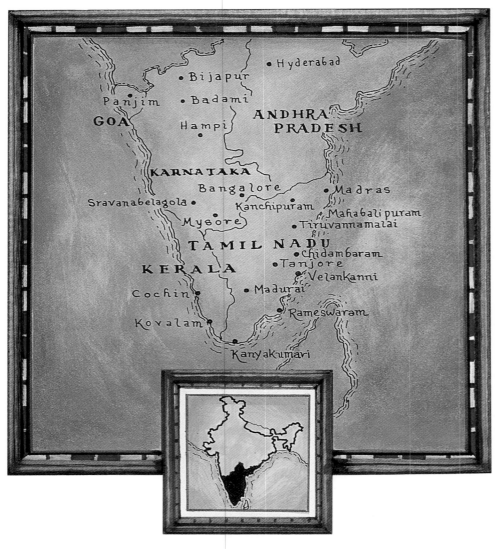

◁ *Opposite*
Palace guard standing in front of mural.
Maharaja's Palace. Mysore, Karnataka.

The South: Goa, Karnataka, Andhra Pradesh, Kerala and Tamil Nadu

South India was never conquered by the invading Muslims. Its culture is discernibly different from the North. The most predominant landmarks of the South are the huge temples with their multi-storied gates. Most of the restaurants are vegetarian, meat having been introduced into northern diets by the Muslims. Much of the food was cooked with too many hot peppers for me to eat. The reason for the hot spices in the South Indian diet is to promote perspiration, which has a cooling effect on the body in that hot climate.

The transportation system was better organized in the South, and the buses were not nearly as crowded. Boarding was an orderly process.

Kerala, located on the western seaboard fronting the Arabian Sea, is a quiet, rural area where life has a slow pace. It was as if the twentieth century had not yet penetrated the secluded hamlets of that state.

The South

The history of the city of Cochin (Kochi) is of particular interest to Westerners. The city contains the oldest church constructed by Europeans in India. St. Francis Church, built in 1503 by Portuguese Franciscan friars, is in excellent condition and still in use. Cochin also is home to a 16th century synagogue, one of the most important in Asia. Both Jews and Christians, however, settled on the Malabar coast long before the Middle Ages.

The modern cities of Bangalore and Mysore in the state of Karnataka are cosmopolitan. That state's magnificent Hoysala temples and the archaeological sites of Hampi and Badami are worth visiting, as are the colossal temples of Tamil Nadu.

The best known city in Andhra Pradesh is its capital of Hyderabad. The state has an interesting array of Muslim, Buddhist and Hindu sites, including the holy mountain of Tirumala which is accessible from Madras.

Most foreign travelers go to Goa to enjoy the superb white sand beaches and crystal-clear turquoise water, but the small enclave's Portuguese heritage is also noteworthy.

Goa: Portuguese Splendor of the Past

The Portuguese arrived in Goa in 1510. With the exception of a brief occupation by the British during the Napoleonic Wars in Europe, they maintained their hegemony until 1961, when India expelled them. Nonetheless, Goa still maintains its distinctively Portuguese appearance and slow-paced life.

Woman selling textiles from Rajasthan. Market. Anjuna Beach, Goa.

Muslim man with prayer beads. Panjim, Goa.

Main altar, dedicated to St. Catherine of Alexandria. Se Cathedral, Old Goa. Completed in 1652.

Old Goa

Located six miles from the old Portuguese town of Panjim, now the state capital, is the city of Old Goa. During the 16th century, the wealthy Portuguese city grew rapidly, eventually rivaling Lisbon. Large churches, monasteries and convents were built by religious orders who came to Goa under royal mandate. The interiors of some of the churches are as lavish as those of Spain and Portugal. Old Goa's splendor did not last long, for at the end of the 16th century, Portugal's supremacy on the seas was replaced by the English, Dutch and French.

As I approached the city by bus, a thrill went through my body when I caught my first glimpse of the huge white churches extending through the canopy of the lush foliage. It was as if I were entering another era.

The largest church at Old Goa is Se Cathedral. The Portuguese-Gothic structure was begun in 1562 and took more than 55 years to build. To complete the altars took an additional 45 years.

The Church of St. Francis of Assisi was, to me, Goa's most interesting. Built on the site of an earlier chapel constructed by eight Franciscan friars who arrived in 1517, the current building dates to 1661. Two turrets give the church a fortress-like appearance.

The Basilica of Bom Jesus contains the tomb of Goa's patron saint, St. Francis Xavier. He arrived in Goa in 1542 to spread the message of Christianity along the Malabar and Coromandel coasts. His missionary zeal took him to Indonesia, Japan and an island off the coast of China where he died at age 46. His body evidently remained in a state of incorruptibility for perhaps 100 years and he was canonized in 1622. His glass coffin is displayed for public view every 10 years.

Hindu sculptures, mountain-top cave. Badami.

Vishnu enthroned on cosmic serpent Ananta. Cave III, Badami.
Chalukya Dynasty, ca. 578 A.D.

Women washing clothes. Badami.

Badami, Chalukyan capital from mid-6th to mid-8th century.

Golgumbaz, mausoleum of Mohammed Adil Shah. Second largest dome in the world. Bijapur. 17th century.

Nandi (bull), associated with Brahma, Creator of the Universe. Pattadakal.

Children on porch. Religious pictures frame entrance to home. Pattadakal.

Wall frieze depicting king's army. Hazaara Rama Temple. Hampi.

*Mythological animals carved on pillars of
temple. Hampi.*

Sunrise from Matanga Hill. Hampi.

Gopuram (gate), 156 feet high.
Virupaksha Temple. Hampi. Mid-
15th century.

Keshava Vishnu Temple. Hoysala Dynasty, Somnathpur. 1268 A.D.

Somnathpur

Some of India's most famous religious monuments are located in Karnataka. They were built during the Hoysala Dynasty which controlled that region from the 11th to 14th centuries. About 25 miles east of Mysore is the Hoysala temple at Somnathpur, built in the second half of the 13th century. The squat star-shaped temple is one of the more interesting buildings in India. Carved from soapstone, virtually the entire exterior of the relatively small temple is covered with superb sculptures. Because soapstone (steatite) is soft when first quarried, the sculptors were able to carve elaborate details. After a period of exposure to the air, the material hardens and turns dark.

Man selling strung marigolds to be used as malas (religious garlands). Market. Mysore.

Dancing woman. Kasava Temple, Belur.
1117 A.D.

Belur/Halebid

North of Mysore are two temples built during the same period. Describing the Hoysala temple at Belur, the 19th century critic, Fergusson, was quoted as saying, "...these friezes...carved with a minute elaboration of detail...are one of the most marvelous exhibitions of human labor to be found even in the patient East."[1]

Ten miles from Belur is the Hoysala temple at Halebid, considered by art historians to contain the best examples of Medieval Indian sculpture.

Woman with mirror. Kasava Temple,
Belur. 1117 A.D.

Sravanabelagola

One of the oldest and most important Jain pilgrimage centers is located at Sravanabelagola. The temple is built on top of a hill and famous for its huge statue of Lord Bahubali (Gomateshvara). The 51 feet high figure of the Jain saint can be seen from a distance of 15 miles. Carved from a single rock, it is said to be the world's tallest monolithic statue. The word "Sravanabelagola" means "the monk on the top of the hill."

In 1981, a special ceremony which is held every 12 to 14 years coincided with the 1,000th anniversary of the installation of the statue. As a result, over one million people attended, necessitating the construction of several towns to accommodate the vast numbers. The excursion to the three Hoysala temples and Sravanabelagola was one of the more impressive conducted tours of my entire trip, and I would highly recommend it.

Pilgrims, devotees of Shiva. Karnataka.

Kerala

Foreigners have been coming to Kerala for thousands of years. As a result, the culture of this state has a cosmopolitan blend. The Phoenicians came in search of spices, sandalwood and ivory. They were followed by the Romans. Later the Arabs came and dominated spice shipments to Europe. Kerala fishermen still use huge cantilevered fishing nets introduced by the Chinese. Winding streets are lined with Portuguese-style houses which were built as early as the 15th century. Traditional South Indian Kathakali dance-dramas, which date back 500 years, may be seen in the evenings. Their Hindu stories are based on the <u>Ramayana</u> and <u>Mahabharata</u>.

Kerala has an unusual mixture of religions. About 20 percent are Christians, who are mainly concentrated in the central part of the state. Hindus constitute about 60 percent of the population and live primarily in the south; Muslims comprise about 20 percent and live mostly in the north. The state's 91 percent literacy rate is the highest in India, well above the national average of 55 percent.

Christianity had already arrived in India 1,400 years before Vasco da Gama sailed around the southern cape of Africa and landed at nearby Calicut in 1498. It is said that the Apostle St. Thomas arrived here in 52 A.D., which means Christianity was established in Kerala earlier than most other places in the world. The earliest Christian communities were Syrian Orthodox, which were there at least as early as 190 A.D. When the Portuguese arrived, they were surprised to find that Christian communities already existed. Because these Christians had never heard of the Pope and were not under his authority, the Portuguese tried to suppress their activities. In spite of their efforts many Syrian Orthodox churches are still active in Kerala today.

It cannot be documented when the first Jews arrived in Kerala, though probably they came with King Solomon's merchant fleet. Some historians believe that the earliest Jews to settle there were descendants of the Jews taken to Babylon by Nebuchadnezzar, and there is ethnomusicological evidence to support that claim. Some scholars think that they once numbered tens of thousands. Their descendants have intermarried with the Hindu population, though there is still a small community of European Jews, many of whom probably came from Spain.

Cochin

The synagogue was built in 1568 and is said to be the oldest in the British Commonwealth. The European Jewish community that lived around the synagogue since the 16th century once numbered perhaps 4,000, but today most of the younger Jews have gone to Israel and only a few families remain.

Though most Jews have left India, their immigration to Israel was not motivated by intolerance or discrimination, but by a desire to live in the Jewish state. The Jews were the first large group of foreigners to settle in India and they were given a land grant. Because successive Hindu rulers were hospitable to them, India broadened her reputation as a land of tolerance.

It was the Jewish holiday of Passover when I visited the synagogue, and only seven persons attended the evening service. The synagogue's floor consisted of hundreds of 18th century Chinese blue and white porcelain tiles from Canton, which seemed much too fine to walk upon. Hanging from the ceiling were many crystal chandeliers.

Returning to my hotel one evening, I came upon a Durga dance celebration, honoring God as Divine Mother. It looked similar to a Mardi Gras procession in New Orleans, with bearers holding lights so all could see the street dancers. A few of the dancers seemed to be in a trance, and placed flames in their mouths or pierced their tongues with long metal rods. If their feats were not drug induced, it was an impressive demonstration of faith and devotion. Not being interested in those types of practices, I did not watch very long.

Synagogue, Cochin. Built in 1568.

Porcelain tiles with blue underglaze. Chinese, Canton. 18th century. Floor of synagogue, Cochin.

Fishing nets. Kovalam Beach. Kerala.

Kovalam

Many say that Kovalam has India's most scenic beach, and based on the few that I visited, I would agree.

Kovalam is on the western seaboard of Kerala. It lies just south of the town of Trivandrum, and is about a two hour bus ride north of Kanyakumari. Its two main coves are bordered with palms and separated from one another by a rocky promontory. Kovalam is a fishing village. The fishermen still use dugouts to take their nets out into the Arabian Sea, and pull them in by hand. The villagers work in groups similar to cooperatives, and divide the catch among themselves. I was surprised at the number of large fish in each haul.

Kovalam is a sleepy little hamlet, still unspoiled by Western culture. The local farmers grow rice, fruits and vegetables, and life goes on as it always has. I stayed there for four days, enjoying the food and the sun.

Cantilevered fishing nets said to be introduced by Chinese traders from the court of Kublai Khan. Cochin, Kerala.

Madras

Madras is India's fourth largest city and is the capital of Tamil Nadu. Portions of the city along the Bay of Bengal have large open areas. Many of the municipal buildings combine features of Hindu and Islamic architecture, blended with more recent British elements. Their exotic appearance is similar to the "onion domes" of Red Square in Moscow. The museum has an excellent collection of Chola bronze statuary (10th-12th century).

Kanchipuram

Kanchipuram is one of the seven sacred cities of India and served as capital of three successive kingdoms. The giant *gopurams* (gates) of the spectacular temple complexes can be seen from miles away. Their sight invoked a feeling of awe, and I could imagine that my response had been shared by many of those who had approached the temples which were over a thousand years old.

Huge temples are located throughout the city. The Pallava, Cholas and Vijayanagar kings who constructed them evidently enjoyed building on a large scale. One of the gates at a Shiva temple is 192 feet tall. Massive stone walls enclosed over 22 acres. Inside, there were large rectangular pools of water for purification rites. Some of the temples had halls with a thousand pillars. At a temple dedicated to Vishnu, each of the thousand pillars was artistically carved with that deity riding on a horse.

Dancing Shiva and elephant-headed Ganesh. Ekambareshwara Temple, Kanchipuram.

Vishnu mounted on horse, Vaikuntaperumal Temple. Construction begun 674 A.D., completed 800 A.D. Kanchipuram.

"The Descent of the Ganges From Heaven." Mahabalipuram. Pallava Dynasty, 7th - 8th century A.D.

Mahabalipuram

Mahabalipuram (Mamallapuram) is about 37 miles south of Madras. It served as the second capital and seaport of the Pallava kings, the first Tamil dynasty of consequence. Among the many important sites to visit is an immense relief carved on the face of a huge rock. The carving depicts the descent to earth of the sacred river Ganges through the matted locks of Shiva's hair. It contains over 100 figures of gods, men and animals.

At the southern edge of Mahabalipuram is a group of five free-standing temples, four of them carved from the same long granite boulder. They are called *rathas*, meaning chariot, and are "vehicles" to God. Built during the 7th - 8th centuries, they are replicas of ancient wooden structures and are the architectural prototypes of the mammoth South Indian temples which dominate the landscape of Tamil Nadu.

Located near the ocean is the Shore Temple. It is the earliest known example of a stone-built temple in the South. Erected on granite blocks, it has a soaring tower. Its design strongly influenced the architecture of the Cholas, who succeeded the Pallavas as the dominant dynasty in the Tamil region. On the evening I was there, its tiered pyramidal tower made a stunning silhouette against a bright red-orange sunset.

Shore Temple at sunset. Mahabalipuram.

Tamil Nadu

Shiva-Parvati Temple, at the base of the holy mountain of Arunachala. Tiruvannamalai.

Fort overlooking rice fields. Gingee.

Pottery horses which serve as guardians of village. Near Gingee.

Bride at marriage ceremony. Gingee.

Bride sitting on back of old Morris Minor Convertible which is mounted with flashing lights and used especially for weddings.

Roof finial, Hindu temple.
Chidambaram.

Chidambaram

Chidambaram was a Chola capital from 907 to 1310. From miles away, I could see the huge temple complex dedicated to Nataraja, the dancing Shiva who dissolves all of the world back into the One. Two of the huge pyramid-like *gopurams* (gates) are almost 150 feet high and are carved with the 108 classical postures of Nataraja in his role of cosmic dancer. The complex, which covers over 32 acres, is said to be the oldest in the South. It is considered the Mt. Kailasa (the snow white Himalayan summit which is the mystical abode of Shiva) of South India.

The fire ceremony conducted in the late afternoon was theatrical. The priest used a large candelabrum with many candles to illuminate an image of the dancing Nataraja. The priest's rhythmic arm movements were made more dramatic by the musical accompaniment of a drum and horn. At moments of intensity, bells were rung.

In many restaurants in South India, dish washing is kept to a minimum. My lunch and dinner were served on a palm leaf. The diner pours a little water on it to wash the surface and the excess is poured on the floor.

Gopuram (gate) at sunset, Nataraja Temple. Chidambaram, 10th century. A.D.

Rajarajeshvara Temple. Tanjore. Chola Dynasty, ca. 1,000 A.D.

Tirujnana Samanda, one of the 62 Shiva saints, as a dancing child. Bronze, ca. 14th - 15th century. Art Gallery, Tanjore.

Elephant representing Lord Ganesh, blessing boy with his trunk. Rajarajeshvara Temple. Tanjore.

Tanjore

The famous Chola temple in Tanjore was built about 1000 A.D. It is the masterpiece of South Indian architecture. The pyramidal tower rises over the main shrine to a height of 206 feet. It is topped with an 81 ton domed capstone, which was raised into place by an earth ramp, similar to those used by the Egyptians. The inner courtyard is guarded by one of India's largest Nandis (Shiva's bull), which also is carved from a single rock.

In the afternoon, I went to a famous Shiva temple located eight miles away at Thiruvaiyaru. While pilgrims were worshiping at an altar, a priest abruptly closed a curtain, concealing it from view. The priest was symbolically showing us how God plays "hide and seek" with His devotees.

A woman who spoke no English approached me and led me to an obscure shrine where the priest was performing the fire ritual. As I left the temple, the woman indicated I should follow her. I had no idea what she wanted as we walked for over half a mile. Several times I considered turning back because it was getting dark and I was ready to return to Tanjore. We finally reached a small building and immediately upon entering, I could feel spiritual vibrations pouring into my body. I was puzzled by the experience. A young priest came out and explained to me that this was the shrine of Sri Tyagaraja (1767-1847), a famous saint who is said to be the greatest musical composer of South India. Aside from being a musical prodigy, he had attained *samadhi*, the highest conscious union with God. Through God's grace, I had been able to feel his vibrations, though at the time I did not even know who he was!

The woman led me to the bus stop for Tanjore. As we *pranamed* to each other, I was grateful to both her and God for this most unexpected blessing.

Healing Miracles at Velankanni

Pilgrims of all religions flock to a Roman Catholic church because of the many miraculous healings which have taken place there. It is the Church of Our Lady of Good Health, located 55 miles southeast of Tanjore in the town of Velankanni.

The huge church is dedicated to Mary, Mother of Jesus. Towards the end of the 17th century, a Portuguese ship was about to capsize in a violent storm when Mary appeared and saved the sailors from drowning. Other sightings of Mary and Baby Jesus occurred close by, and a shrine now marks one of the locations.

The large chapel dedicated to Mary was filled with praying devotees of various faiths. Some Indians removed their shoes in the church (probably Hindus), others did not. The ecumenical gathering inspired me, foreshadowing the peace yet possible in today's world.

The object of veneration was a statue of Mary holding the Baby Jesus. Both Mary and the Infant Christ were wrapped in orange cloth, which only exposed their faces. Each wore a regal red crown, richly ornamented with gold. A variety of jeweled ornaments hanging from the image of Mary looked like fetishes. The effigy could have been equally at home in any religion which uses icons.

A museum to honor the numerous healings which had taken place was located next door to the church. Glass cases displayed letters attesting to the particular healing which occurred. Many had enclosed gold or silver replicas of the cured body parts. Some sent jewelry or other offerings.

I, too, received a physical healing at Velankanni. For the previous two weeks, I had been having terrible stomach pains every time I ate, and I was deeply concerned about my condition. After leaving the museum, I noticed that I had no ill effects when I ate the food I purchased for my two hour bus ride back to Tanjore. From that day to this, I have never again had stomach pains. Thinking back to that morning in Velankanni, I remember the exact moment when God responded to my tearful prayer.

Madurai

The famous Shree Meenakshi Temple attracts thousands of visitors a day. The temple covers about 15 acres in the middle of the city and draws pilgrims from all over India. Its enormous 150 feet high, nine story tall gate is covered with brightly painted gods, goddesses and animals.

One afternoon I went to the Gandhi Museum. Because of my reverence for the "Father of Modern India," I visited as many sites associated with Gandhi as possible. The museum displayed his blood-stained *dhoti* which he was wearing on the day that he was assassinated. When the great man fell dying to the ground, his last earthly act was to raise his hand in a peaceful gesture, blessing his assailant.

Pilgrims, Ayyappa sect from Kerala.
Bazaar, Meenakshi Temple. Madurai.

Sculptural detail, South Gopuram
(gate). Meenakshi Temple, Madurai.
Nayak Dynasty, 17th century.

West Gopuram (gate), Meenakshi Temple. Madurai. Nayak Dynasty, 17th century.

Tamil Nadu

Rameswaram

En route to the southern tip of India, I visited the pilgrimage center of Rameswaram, located on an island in the Gulf of Mannar. The town of 33,000 has one of the most important temples in the South, which is a fine example of Dravidian architecture. Construction was begun in the 12th century A.D., though additions were made over succeeding centuries. Its magnificent corridors are lined with finely carved pillars. One of the corridors is 4,000 feet long — the longest in India.

Kanyakumari: Where Three Oceans Meet

Kanyakumari is the southernmost point of India, and is where the Bay of Bengal, Indian Ocean and Arabian Sea merge. It was here that I visited a special Gandhi Memorial. A portion of the great saint's ashes had been enshrined on a pedestal prior to being placed in the ocean there. Peaceful emanations marked the spot where his ashes once sat. Such is the legacy of those who have known peace.

Built 200 yards off shore and on two rocky islands is the Vivekananda Memorial. The imposing beauty of the island temple is enhanced by its natural setting. Built in 1970, the temple incorporates architectural styles from all over India. At the base of the dark rocky island, white waves broke gently upon massive boulders. As the afternoon sun set on the temple's stone surface, its central dome and upper portions glowed a soft mauve.

The temple honors the swami, who went there in 1892 to meditate, before leaving for the West to share the wisdom of Hinduism. Foremost disciple of the great Indian sage Sri Ramakrishna, Swami Vivekananda had been invited to attend the World Parliament of Religions convened in Chicago in September, 1893.

Vivekananda Memorial, Kanyakumari. Built in 1970.

The swami received an overwhelming response from the audience of 7,000 and brought them to their feet when he said:

Sisters and Brothers of America, it fills my heart with joy unspeakable to rise in response to the warm and cordial welcome which you have given us. I thank you in the name of the most ancient order of monks in the world; I thank you in the name of the mother of all religions, and I thank you in the name of the millions and millions of Hindu people of all classes and sects. I am proud to belong to a religion which has brought the world both tolerance and universal acceptance. We believe not only in universal tolerance but we accept all religions to be true.

Dancing Shiva (Nataraja), who dissolves all things back into the One as He dances to the cosmic rhythms. Bronze. Chola Dynasty, 11th - 12th century. Art Gallery, Tanjore.

Epilogue

The German philosopher Goethe said that to live in another's country and to speak another's language increases one's knowledge ten-fold. I certainly would agree. Our shrinking world makes it easier today than ever before to adopt the best from all civilizations. Certainly no nation or religion has a monopoly on truth. West and East have much to share.

Of all of the nations in the world, India is the most spiritually blessed. More and more Americans are learning that materialism does not give lasting satisfaction, and they are turning to India for spiritual guidance.

The most sublime purpose of religion is to teach how to know God. Once we become aware of the spark of God (the soul) within us, we realize that we are all interconnected children of the Most High. Then we understand there is but one religion with many denominations. All religions lead to God and it does not matter which path one follows: the multicolored lamps of each faith burn with the same white flame.

I do not suggest that the various forms of religious worship be made homogeneous, for each appeals to the particular culture to which it was brought. Rituals and symbols may vary, but the principles they represent are universal. Once we experience the God within, religious prejudice disappears.

I believe that religion should offer a scientific basis by which the practitioner may know God. Yoga meditation is the scientific way to experience God-communion. By consciously withdrawing the mind from the restless senses, one's attention can be placed upon God. Meditation makes God knowable to ordinary people through the framework of their existing religion. The Bible says: "Be still, and know that I am God" (Psalms 46:10). Once the mind becomes calm, the image of the Divine is reflected within.

When Albert Einstein said, "Science without religion is lame, and religion without science is blind," he could have been describing contemporary America and India. India has become over-balanced spiritually and cannot adequately provide for the material needs of its own people. America leads the world in consumer comforts, but has veered sharply off course morally. Each culture would benefit from adopting the best qualities of the other. It is my belief that the United States and India can give the world a new direction: a materially efficient democracy that is spiritually guided. For this to become a reality, each of us must do our part.

Chapter Notes

Introduction

1. Paramahansa Yogananda, "Thou hast many Names," <u>Whispers from Eternity</u> (Los Angeles: Self-Realization Fellowship, 1959), 143.

Chapter Two: The East

1. Located in downtown Calcutta, the temple is believed to be about 200 years old. It also is known as Kalighat, and should not be confused with Kali Temple associated with Sri Ramakrishna, located in the suburb of Dakshineswar.

2. The sixth century B.C. saw the birth of many extraordinary spiritual and philosophical geniuses: Confucius and Lao-tzu in China, Pythagoras and Heraclitus in Greece, the Hebrew prophet Zechariah, the Jain prophet Mahavira and the Upanishadic sages in India.

Chapter Three: The North

1. Sri Daya Mata, "The Inner Paradise of Even-Mindedness," <u>Self-Realization</u> (Los Angeles: Self-Realization Fellowship, Spring, 1991), 10-12.

2. Paramahansa Yogananda, <u>Autobiography of a Yogi</u> (Los Angeles: Self-Realization Fellowship, 1985), 389.

3. Sri Gyanamata, <u>God Alone</u> (Los Angeles: Self-Realization Fellowship, 1984), 26.

4. The following story has been summarized from Ananda K. Coomaraswamy and Sister Nivedita, <u>Myths of Hindus and Buddhists</u> (New York: Dover Publications, 1967), 369-370.

Chapter Five: The West

1. The spiritually advanced yogi probably had attuned his consciousness with God, and could heal others in accordance with Divine Will. What herb or medicine he gave to them is of no importance, but probably served to awaken their greater faith.

Chapter Six: The South

1. James Fergusson, <u>History of Indian and Eastern Architecture</u>, Vol. II (New York, 1899), 7-20.

◁ *Opposite*
Sunset. Indian Ocean. Kanyakumari,
Tamil Nadu.

Glossary*

Aryans. Second millennium B.C. invaders of northwestern India from Central Asia. The term also applies to a language family now known as Indo-European.

ashram. A spiritual residence. The Hindu equivalent of a monastery or hermitage.

Aum (Om). The basis of all sounds and universal symbol word for God. *Aum* of the Vedas became the sacred word *Hum* to the Tibetans; *Amin* to the Moslems; and *Amen* of the Egyptians, Greeks, Romans, Jews and Christians. *Aum* is the all-pervading sound emanating from the Holy Ghost; the "Word" of the Bible; the voice of creation testifying to the Divine Presence in every atom.

avatar. A soul who has attained union with Spirit and then returns to earth to help humankind; a divine incarnation.

Bhakti Yoga. (Devotion). The path to God which emphasizes all-surrendering love and adoration as the principal means for communion and union with God.

Bodhisattva. (Buddhism). One who has almost attained the state of *nirvana* (liberation) but who renounces it and retains his human form on earth to help others.

darshan. (Holy sight). A special blessing received from seeing a holy person. Visiting a holy site where a saint has been or where sacred relics are contained also is considered *darshan*.

dharma. Eternal principles of righteousness that upholds all creation; humankind's inherent duty to live in harmony with these principles.

dhoti. Male garment knotted around the waste, similar to a *lungi* (sarong), but cloth is pulled up between the legs.

Dravidian. A term applied to the peoples and languages of South India. The Dravidians were the predominant power of India prior to ascendancy of the Aryans, who drove them to South India. The core of Hinduism is probably the religion of the inhabitants of the Indus Valley whom many believe were the Dravidians.

ghat. Long rows of steps leading down to a river which facilitate devotees getting to the water.

guru. (Spiritual teacher). When devotees are earnest in their search for God, the Lord sends them a guru. The guru is much more than just an ordinary teacher. He is a living manifestation of scriptural truths and is able to guide and direct his disciples to final realization. Without a guru, the ordinary person will never attain Self-realization. Today in the West, the word guru has been corrupted to mean "a teacher with a large following."

Indo-Aryan. A branch of the Indo-European language family that includes the languages of Pakistan and Northern India, such as classical Sanskrit and modern Hindi. The earliest Indo-Aryan language was Sanskrit. The linguistic term sometimes is applied to Indo-European-speaking people who entered the Indian subcontinent from Central Asia about 1500 B.C.

Jnana Yoga. (Wisdom). The path to union with God by transforming the discriminative power of the intellect into the all-knowing wisdom of the soul.

*Many of the metaphysical definitions are based on glossaries in Self-Realization Fellowship's books by Paramahansa Yogananda, such as <u>Man's Eternal Quest</u> and <u>Where There Is Light</u>.

Glossary

karma. (Effects of past action). The law of *karma* is the effect of an individual's past actions, which may be from this life or previous lifetimes. Every religion in the world teaches a similar concept of action and reaction, cause and effect, or sowing and reaping.

Any action a person commits, whether it be good or bad, sets in motion a similar pattern of occurrences that will inexorably return like a boomerang to the doer in the present or a future existence. Thus each person becomes the creator of his or her own destiny. What the Western mind views as "fate" would be looked upon by the Hindu as moral consequence. Once one understands that *karma* is the universe's law of justice, an individual accepts responsibility for his or her circumstances and no longer harbors resentments against God or man.

The collective actions of people within communities, countries or the world create *mass karma*, which produces local or global consequences depending on the preponderance of good or evil committed. The thoughts and actions of every person, therefore, are important and contribute to maintaining the well-being of the world.

Karma Yoga. (Service). The path to union with God through selfless service, performing all work and actions with an attitude of non-attachment. By seeing God as the sole Doer and giving the results of one's actions to Him, an individual may become freed from the bondage of the ego.

Krishna. The eighth incarnation of Vishnu who is often colored blue, the color of infinity. Krishna is the most popular Indian deity whose counsel to his disciple Arjuna is given in India's most beloved scripture the Bhagavad Gita. The central message of the Gita is that men and women may attain liberation through love for God, wisdom and performance of right actions in the spirit of non-attachment.

lingam. A phallic shrine object, usually carved of stone, which represents Shiva's (the third aspect of the Hindu Trinity) creative role within the universe.

lungi. Sarong-like clothing worn by men.

mahasamadhi. The last meditation or conscious communion with God, known beforehand to a perfected master, when he merges himself in the Holy Spirit or cosmic sound of *Aum* or Amen as he gives up his physical body. From the Sanskrit *maha*, "great," and *samadhi*, state of God union.

mantra. Sacred root word sounds which have a spiritually beneficial vibratory effect upon the person who repeats them.

master. One who has attained self-mastery, as evidenced by the ability to enter at will the breathless state of *sabikalpa samadhi* or the higher state of immutable bliss of *nirbikalpa samadhi*.

Mughal. (Also spelled Moghul). The Muslim dynasty of Indian emperors. The six greatest were Babur, Humayun, Akbar, Jehangir, Shah Jahan and Aurangzeb. These six ruled from 1527 to 1707.

pranam. A ritual gesture of respect performed by placing the fingers and palms of both hands together and slightly bowing the head. To some it means "My soul bows to your soul."

pranayama. The conscious control of *prana* (life energy), or currents of subtle energy flows in the body which activate and sustain life.

prashad. Food (sweets, fruit, etc.) offered to a deity or living saint, which is sanctified because it has been blessed. It is distributed by priests in the temples and may be eaten there or taken away to share with others.

Glossary

Raja Yoga. (The "royal" road). The path to union with God considered by Krishna in the Bhagavad Gita to be the highest path. It incorporates the most effective methods from the other yoga paths, and teaches that scientific meditation is the basis for God-realization. *Raja Yoga* leads to perfect development of body, mind and soul.

reincarnation. A doctrine which states that human beings who die with unfulfilled material desires have to return to earth again and again, until they are able to reclaim their divine status as children of God.

sadhu. An anchorite; one devoted to asceticism and spiritual discipline.

Sanskrit. The classical and sacred language of India. The oldest form of the Indo-Aryan languages.

spiritual eye. Located at the point between the eyebrows, it is where devotees concentrate their attention when meditating. The spiritual eye is the entryway through which the yogi or yogini passes his or her consciousness into the higher realms and experiences the "Father," "Son," and "Holy Ghost." Jesus spoke of the divine light that is perceived through the spiritual eye when He said: "When thine eye is single [if the two physical eyes focus into the one spiritual eye], thy whole body also is full of light....Take heed therefore that the light which is in thee by not darkness" (Luke 11:34-35). Hindu women mark the spiritual eye on their foreheads with a red "spot" which is known as a *bindi* or *tilak*. The spiritual eye usually is portrayed on the images of saints.

Sri. A title of respect which means "holy" or "revered" when used before the name of a religious person. In the South, the anglicized spelling becomes Shree and in West India, it is spelled Shri.

Sufism. The mystical teachings of Islam whose forms vary across the Islamic world.

swami. A monk who is a member of India's (and the world's) most ancient monastic order, which was reorganized by Swami Shankara in the ninth century. A swami takes formal vows of poverty (renunciation of worldly possessions and ambitions), celibacy and obedience to spiritual authority. He follows the path of meditation and other spiritual practices, and dedicates himself to service to humanity. The Sanskrit word swami means "he who is one with the Self (*Swa*)."

Trinity. (The threefold nature of Spirit when it manifests creation). The theologies of all major religions agree with the ancient Hindu interpretation that when Spirit manifests creation, It becomes the Trinity: *Sat, Tat, Aum,* or the Father, Son, Holy Ghost. *Sat,* (the Father), in the *impersonal* sense, is God as the Creator existing beyond creation without form. *Tat* (the Son), is God's omnipresent intelligence reflecting in an undisturbed state throughout creation. *Aum* (the Holy Ghost) is the active vibratory creative power of God that objectifies or structures creation.

In Hinduism, the impersonal aspect of God the Father as Creator becomes Brahma, who resides beyond the physical universe of space, time and matter. Vishnu represents the Son, who is the Sustainer or Preserver; and Shiva personifies the third part of the Hindu Trinity, the Holy Ghost who destroys or dissolves all things back into the One.

Yoga. One of six systems of Hindu philosophy. A technique of spiritual and physical training by which the individual soul may be united with Unmanifested Spirit.

yogi. A male practitioner of Yoga.

yogini. A female practitioner of Yoga.

Index

* Indicates that word or term is listed in Glossary.

Index

Index